W9-BLU-649

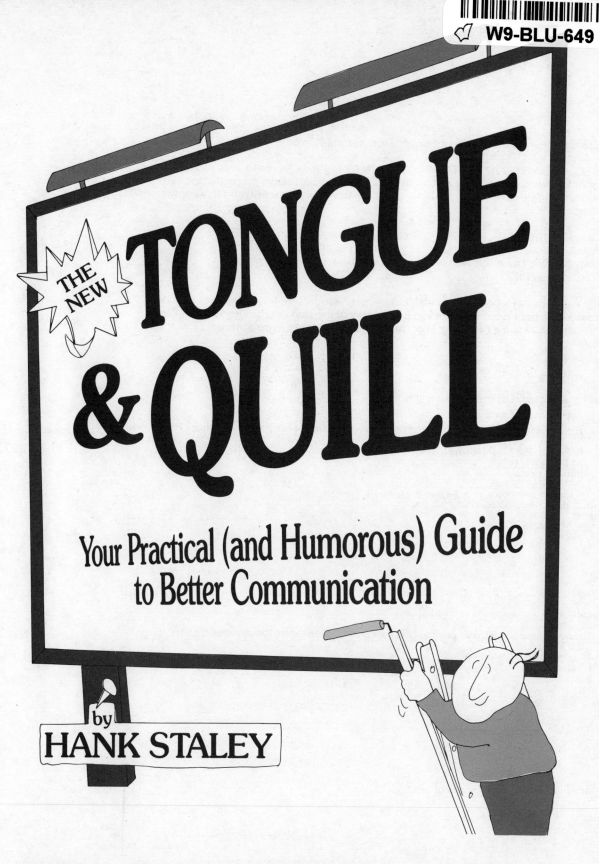

THE NEW TONGUE & QUILL

Your Practical (and Humorous) Guide to Better Communication

by

HANK STALEY

Pergamon-Brassey's International Defense Publishers, Inc.

Washington • New York • London • Oxford
Beijing • Frankfurt • São Paulo • Sydney • Tokyo • Toronto

Copyright © 1990 by Pergamon-Brassey's International Defense Publishers, Inc.

All rights reserved. No part of this book may be reproduced, stored in a retrieval system, or transmitted in any form or by any means—electronic, electrostatic, magnetic tape, mechanical, photocopying, recording, or otherwise—without permission in writing from the publisher.

Editorial Offices
Pergamon-Brassey's
8000 Westpark Drive, 4th Floor
McLean, VA 22102

Order Department
Macmillan Publishing Co.
Front and Brown Streets
Rivderside, NJ 08075

Pergamon-Brassey's books are available at special discounts for bulk purchases for sales promotions, premiums, fund-raising, or educational use through the Special Sales Director, Macmillan Publishing Company, 866 Third Avenue, New York, New York 10022.

Library of Congress Cataloging-in-Publication Data

Staley, H. A.
      The new tongue & quill : your practical (and humorous) guide to better communication / Hank A. Staley.
          p. cm.
      Rev. ed. of: The tongue and quill. 1982.
      Bibliography : p.
      Includes index.
      ISBN 0-08-035975-2 :
      1. Rhetoric.   I. Staley, H. A. Tongue and quill   II. Title.
III. Title: Tongue and quill.
PN187.S67   1989
808'.042—dc20

89-32290
CIP

British Library Cataloguing in Publication Data
Staley, Hank A.
    The new tongue & quill: your practical (and humorous) guide to better communication.
    Hank A. Staley
    1. Verbal communication—Manuals
    I. Title
    808'.1042

ISBN 0-08-035975-2

Published in the United States of America

10   9   8   7   6   5   4   3   2   1

*To Chuck and Ponti, whose gene pool gave me
everything a son could ever want…except height.*

Drawing by Chas. Addams; © 1951, 1979
The New Yorker Magazine, Inc

● ●

Good humor makes all things tolerable.
—Henry Ward Beecher

...even staff communications?
—Herb Schwartz

● ●

PREFACE

This book is for anyone who will ever sling ink at paper, pound a typewriter, punch a keyboard, give a presentation, make a speech, or open his or her mouth in the conduct of tomorrow's business. It's for the executives, secretaries, consultants, tech reps, salespeople, engineers, and teachers of America. It's for private business, the federal sector, high schools, technical schools, and the crowds that populate our campuses from coast to coast. It even reaches beyond our shores since business, government, and education have all become international in scope and impact. In a very practical sense, it's a book for all of us because it's about how we get things done…through communicating.

"We understand you tore the little tag off your mattress."

Saturday Review, 1975

A Publisher's Note

In the past, Brassey's has published several books on communications—about the technology of defense communication systems and about how commanders command and control their troops. *Tongue & Quill* is clearly a major leap for us into a very new area of publishing, a leap that we may not make often. I think it is thus worth briefly explaining to you the reader my personal and commercial reasons for publishing this book when Brassey's normally specializes in the areas of foreign policy, defense, and security.

The personal reason is quite strong. I have known Hank Staley for more than 15 years and consider him a colleague and a good friend. In 1975 Hank worked directly for me as we tried to satisfy a U.S. Air Force need for a course that would prepare captains and majors for their staff responsibilities in higher headquarters after leaving our Air Command and Staff College. As usual, Hank rose to the occasion and created a classic, *The Tongue & Quill: Communicating to Manage in Tomorrow's Air Force.* Now that I am fortunate enough to be a commercial publisher, I felt I should bring Hank's creative and innovative approaches to a broader public. Hank Staley is very special: he is engaging, teaches with humor, enjoys his fellow human beings.

But I must admit to crass commercial motives as well. I don't think there is a publisher in America who wouldn't be tempted to publish a modified, "civilian" version of a book that:

- has almost 2 million copies in circulation,
- had an enormous volume of positive feedback,
- won major prizes, and
- is a lot of fun to read while you learn how to get your point across.

Don't expect this publishing house to publish many books like this one. I do think that, as you get into this special book, you will understand why we wanted to make *Tongue & Quill* available to you.

Franklin D. Margiotta, Ph.D.
President and Director of Publishing

Acknowledgments

My long-held fascination for words found its most dramatic outlet in the earlier award-winning military version of this book. It was an inspiration to watch over two million members of America's most layered bureaucracy praise such a nontraditional approach and style. Over the past thirty years, I have learned that throughout all levels of government, business, and academia there are those who strive to improve their communicative act, those who are already accomplished, and those who are truly lost. The *Tongue & Quill* speaks eyeball-to-eyeball to each of these audiences in a universal language, and every author is obviously indebted to those who use books!

I am also grateful to many personal friends, advisers, and coworkers for past, present, and future successes. Among the most significant would be Frank Margiotta, John Smith, Jana Carter, Charlie Bitner, Jim Delaney, Ildiko Andrews, the folks at Pergamon-Brassey's, and especially, my favorite word wizard, Sallie J. Marks.

CHAPTER 1

The Concept of Communicating

WHAT IT'S ALL ABOUT

What did she say? Does he really mean that? And so it begins. Whether it ends in confusion or clarity is up to us—the communicators. The talkers, the listeners, the writers, the readers are each of us. We make it all happen, and sometimes it doesn't happen the way we'd like it to. Actually, it's impossible *not* to communicate. The only question is, What's the message?

The concept of human communications has been discussed by authors for centuries. Millions of books and billions of words have described and analyzed the process and its impact. These next few pages are definitely not a comprehensive summary of "all that's gone before," but they do offer a sinfully brief refresher on the basic foundations of human communication. And, aside from the fact that we could each profit from an occasional review, this entire book has its roots wrapped around the question of how we communicate with one another and how we can improve that process.

• •

When in Doubt, Mumble.

—book by Dr. James H. Boren
Pres., National Association
of Professional Bureaucrats

• •

TO BEGIN WITH...

Nearly every book on communications gives at least a perfunctory bow to the *critical importance* of the written or spoken word...and even the unspoken signal! Many books, in fact, devote their first chapters to convincing you that human communication (and the intelligence behind it) is all that separates us from the lower forms of animal life. Do you doubt that? Good. Then we can dispense with at least 5,000 words of introduction.

TO ACT, OR NOT TO ACT. THAT IS THE...

Now, the next aspect of the subject normally covers *why* we communicate. The answer is incredibly simple, yet overly creative authors and lecturers can fill books or hours with complex answers. If you burn all that well-intentioned material down to its essential ash, you'll be left with the word "action."

Human communication has no other purpose than to cause some kind of action.

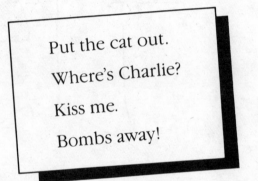

Put the cat out.

Where's Charlie?

Kiss me.

Bombs away!

Do you think we communicate for some reason other than to stimulate overt or mental activity on the part of a listener or reader? Give me an example.

...that's what I thought.

WHAT REALLY HAPPENS?

Somewhere in this hypothetical stack of communications books will be a detailed explanation of the *mechanics* of what happens when we communicate. Scientific, sociological, or technical jargon will blossom like weeds in a melon patch: receptor, stimulus, symbols, information retrieval, transmit, end-coder, response, feedback, etc. Those are all OK words if they eventually lead to the main point—*we cannot **not***

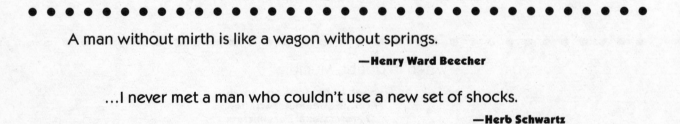

A man without mirth is like a wagon without springs.
—Henry Ward Beecher

...I never met a man who couldn't use a new set of shocks.
—Herb Schwartz

communicate. And when things don't happen the way we plan, it can always be traced to a failure in either the mechanical part of the process ("She's hard of hearing"; "I used unfamiliar words"; etc.) or the psychological part of the process ("I disagreed with his pet idea; he's furious"; "She doesn't like Texans, and I'm from Big D!"). And all of this is relevant only if it opens our eyes to why our communications sometimes go haywire.

TRAPS, BARRIERS, FILTERS, AND THINGS THAT GO BUMP IN THE NIGHT

Communications, whether in the form of a 5-minute phone call or a 50-page report, can go haywire in part (or totally) for a long list of reasons. I'll only cite a few here, however, because the rest of this book is designed to help you remove the barriers and avoid the pitfalls that threaten every one of us when we try to write or speak or listen to each other.

DID YA HEAR THE ONE ABOUT…

…the executive who ordered everyone to answer the phone by first identifying their organization, themselves, and then adding "May I help you, *sir*?" The executive's heart was in the right place, but not the brain. Notwithstanding all the laws and legal precedents about eliminating racist and sexist behavior, it's tough to actually *do* it. We all have our own set of learned barriers to writing or speaking effectively. Some of you reading this now, in fact, still think of a CEO as being a "he," and a nurse as a "she." That's understandable, of course, but not very smart. Inadvertently we exclude members of our audience—and that hurts our communications.

A mentally agile communicator, on the other hand, develops a sixth sense about avoiding ingrained habit traps that allow race, religion, sex, or ethnicity to fog the message. Here are five habit traps that trip up careless communicators:

The Visual Support Trap. Visual aids or illustrations should show examples of all kinds of people who populate America—men, women, folks of different races and ethnic groups, and, where possible, different religious groups. Avoid traditional stereotyping of jobs based on sex or race.

The Religious Trap. Most people have a strong emotional attachment to their spiritual beliefs. Comments like "I jewed them down," or "They were all mackerel snappers," or references to religious events celebrated by only one group, such as Christmas, can leave some readers or listeners with a feeling of exclusion or ridicule.

The Ethnic/Racial Trap. Using words and phrases like "Mexican standoff," "chiefs and Indians," "black hats and white hats" (bad guys and good guys), etc., can be counter-productive. Joke telling is the most common instance when otherwise sensitive people make mistakes. Humor is not universal, and some jokes are only funny depending on the listener's personal frame of reference. In our struggle to improve communications, the only truly effective way to avoid this trap is to retire *any* jokes, phrases, or words that contain ethnic or racial bias.

The Sexist Trap. We tumble into this one repeatedly. Fortunately, we're making progress in eliminating the use of "he," "him," "his," "men," and "man" as general terms applying to *all* humans. We are also graduating from the cumbersome use of "he/she," "him/her," etc. That convention merely highlighted the attitude we were seeking to avoid! Frequently the use of "he/she" can be struck from the sentence, and you find they were only extra words. Where they can't be struck, a specific title like director or chairperson might be suitable. Finally, when titles aren't adequate, plural nouns can solve the problem.

The Translation Trap. How would you like to be a company rep in South America trying to sell Chevy Novas where the literal translation of Nova is "no go!"? Common words, logos, brand names, etc., often have completely different meanings in another language.

While the above traps aren't all inclusive, they should sensitize you to the issues. Everyone who is no longer excluded by our bad communicative habits becomes part of our new audience…and that's the whole point! So much for traps; let's look for barriers.

STATUS RESTRICTS US

Heading the list of barriers, especially for members of large bureaucracies, is status or rank. Too many of us become tongue-tied when communicating with those senior in status and cursory or impatient with those junior in status. This can really gum up the communicative

machinery. We must constantly remind ourselves that we are all "communicative equals" and strive to be candid, direct, and respectful with everyone. Don't allow status to "filter out" important information.

FAILURE TO FIGHT FOR FEEDBACK

The weakest writers and poorest speakers can frequently salvage their crippled communications if they will seek *feedback*. (The best communicators make a habit of doing this.) Ask questions of your audience if you are the communicator; i.e., "Do you really understand this proposal?" "I know I haven't covered this completely—what issues are still fuzzy?" If you are the audience, ask to have the key information repeated if you have any doubt; i.e., "If I understand what you're asking, Mr. Bozworth, you want us to. . . ." Never be shy about confirming what you think are the key points. In nearly every case, the "sender" will be flattered (and impressed) with your desire to fully understand his or her communication. When we fail to make "fightin' for feedback" a consistent habit, we often bump into this next barrier…

ANSWERING THE WRONG QUESTION

Time and again our efforts crash and burn because we never *carefully read* the words or *attentively listen* to the speaker for the real message—for the specific question! Most executives will tell you that "failing to answer the question" is one of the two primary reasons reports, correspondence packages, or studies are dumped back into the laps of hapless employees.

• •

He was all mach and no compass heading.

—some fighter pilot

• •

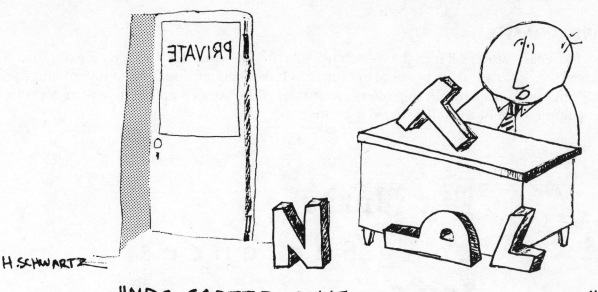

"MRS. CARTER, COME IN AND TAKE A LETTER".

...AIN'T GOT NO PROBLEMS WITH MECHANIX

The other primary reason our efforts turn into paper boomerangs is sloppy mechanics—terrible grammar, inaccurate punctuation, lazy spelling. Searching for educational scapegoats, on which to pin the sad tale of America's declining ability to write and speak acceptable English, is fruitless. If you have a problem with our language, solve it. Self-study or formal course work is the only solution, and there are excellent books and courses available. At a minimum, you should carefully examine the grammar and mechanics chapter of this book. It's a speedy reference worth its weight in platinum paper clips!

GRAMMAR ISN'T *MY* JOB

Don't pawn off your grammar problems on the secretary, clerk-typist, or word processing center! Our research tells us that more and more typists (be it right or wrong) are typing *exactly what they see on the drafts*—they haven't the time, the talent, or the inclination to wet-nurse weak writers back to grammatical health.

When it comes to the spoken word, of course, we don't even have the secretary to lean on! We can hide our spelling problems, but we totally expose our ability to organize, pronounce, and persuade effectively without annoying mannerisms and verbal stumbles. Acceptable English is our job—no one else's—and it should be a source of pride for each of us. Here, again, you'll find help in the grammar and mechanics chapter.

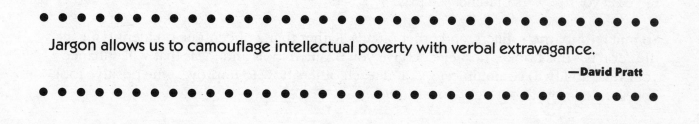

Jargon allows us to camouflage intellectual poverty with verbal extravagance.

—**David Pratt**

BUREAUBAFFLE

This is the last barrier I'll mention here, and, like the first one, it is a serious disease for many writers and speakers, particularly those in federal government, the military, and the social, medical, and engineering sciences. Bureaubaffle is a viral epidemic with any one or a combination of the following symptoms:

Big Words
Long Sentences
JaR Gon
and lots of passive voice

Anytime you have to say "Huh?" after reading something or listening to someone, you can be positive the bureaubaffle bug has bitten.

Unlike malaria, however, bureaubaffle is easy to cure. In fact, it's the easiest affliction to eliminate among all the diseases that frequently befall communicators. Once you learn to spot the obvious symptoms, your scalpel-wielding skill will become legend! Shrink the big words, chop the foot-long sentences, convert the jargon to words you know your audience will understand, and activate the passive voice. (More on that later!) That's all there is to it.

LIMPING LOGIC

Nothing cripples a clearly written, properly punctuated paper quicker than a fractured fact or a distorted argument. Avoiding this pitfall is the most difficult, even for good writers and speakers. Logic is tough to teach, and learn, because it occupies the uppermost rung in human capacity—the ability to think in the abstract. We slip into bad habits at an early age, and it takes some doing to alter our habitual approach to problem solving. (Tune in to step three of the six-step checklist for some useful words on how to increase your powers of logic! See page 37.)

So much for barriers, filters, and other pitfalls. Rather than concentrate on identifying all the "don'ts," this book is designed to give you positive tools and ideas that will enhance your own ability to communicate. . .and teach others how to improve. One positive tool you should know about right now is *time*.

WHEN TIME TRANSFORMS THE MESSAGE

Since you've just read about a variety of barriers, perhaps you've gotten the impression that communicating successfully merely consists of making sure you remove the barriers and clean up your logic. Right? Not necessarily. Legitimate disagreements or unalterably opposed viewpoints are to be expected, *even when the communication is thoroughly effective in design and execution.* Then does that mean your communication is doomed to fail because it runs counter to current philosophy or a particular viewpoint? Again, the answer is "Not necessarily." There is a phenomenon known as the *time dimension* in human communications. This simply means that although your message was rejected, it was heard and understood nevertheless. You planted a seed with your communication, and that seed might germinate and be fertilized by other communications that are heard or seen by the target audience. Eventually, that seed (perhaps a new idea you were trying to sell) is accepted by the target audience (. . .your boss, perhaps?).

Nearly 30 years ago Tamotsu Shibutani wrote *Improvised News. . .A Sociological Study of Rumor.* In his book he vividly described the importance of the time dimension. Ideas, once heard, *cannot be erased*, and perceptions are constantly changing. Don't take the initial rejection of your idea as a "failure to communicate." You may be surprised to find the idea accepted after weeks, months, or even years have passed! So, fear not—go forth and plant seeds.

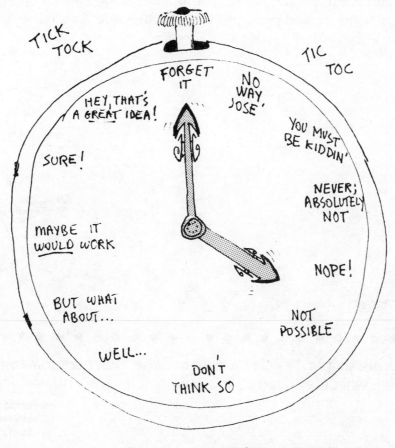

AND . . . AS TIME MARCHES ON . . . .

LOOKING BACK...

When we communicate, our objective is to cause some form of action on the part of the listener or reader. When we failed to get the action we were after, one of two things happened: (1) our communication was flawed in some way—we violated one or more of the basic steps in constructing an effective communication; i.e., hit a barrier, stumbled in our logic, failed to "answer the question," etc.; or (2) our audience simply didn't agree with us. You also read earlier about the basics underlying the why and how of communications and about some of the barriers and pitfalls we may encounter.

This brief introduction is your framework for communicating. Ultimately, these communications issues affect our ability to do our jobs effectively. Although it may seem a gigantic philosophical leap from "success and advancement" to "writing an effective paragraph," reality illustrates the opposite.

The mechanics of writing and speaking are easy to teach if you have the time, and relatively easy to learn if you have the inclination. As this introduction implies, however, the thinking and understanding process is not so easy. How do we improve our ability to think more logically? Some answers to that question are in this book, but be aware that your ego has a high stake in the outcome, and it may take extra effort to swallow that pill. Becoming a better communicator (writer, speaker, or listener) also requires a special sensitivity to situations and people. We'll call this *feedback*. As you'll find out, feedback can be enjoyable, rewarding, and perhaps even startling. You'll also discover it's the last step in the six-step checklist.

● ●

My guidelines are simple. Be selective. Be concise. Don't tell someone what you know; tell them what they need to know, what it means, and why it matters.

—**General David C. Jones
Chairman, Joint Chiefs
of Staff, 1978**

● ●

CHAPTER 2

The Basic Checklist

SIX STEPS TO BETTER COMMUNICATIONS

This chapter discusses those fundamentals of communication that are universal to writing and speaking. The basic philosophy and guidance for more effective writing is just as valid for more effective speaking (. . .and those few fundamentals unique to speaking are in "The Tongue" section).

The checklist below is the key to your future success in preparing any spoken or written communication. The six steps are not always used in sequence, nor are they exclusive of each other; you may want to tailor them to your own style and approach. Nevertheless, the steps will definitely focus your attention on how to increase your success as a communicator.

1. **Analyze purpose and audience**

2. **Conduct the research**

3. **Support your ideas**

4. **Get organized**

5. **Draft and edit with English that's alive**

6. **Fight for feedback**

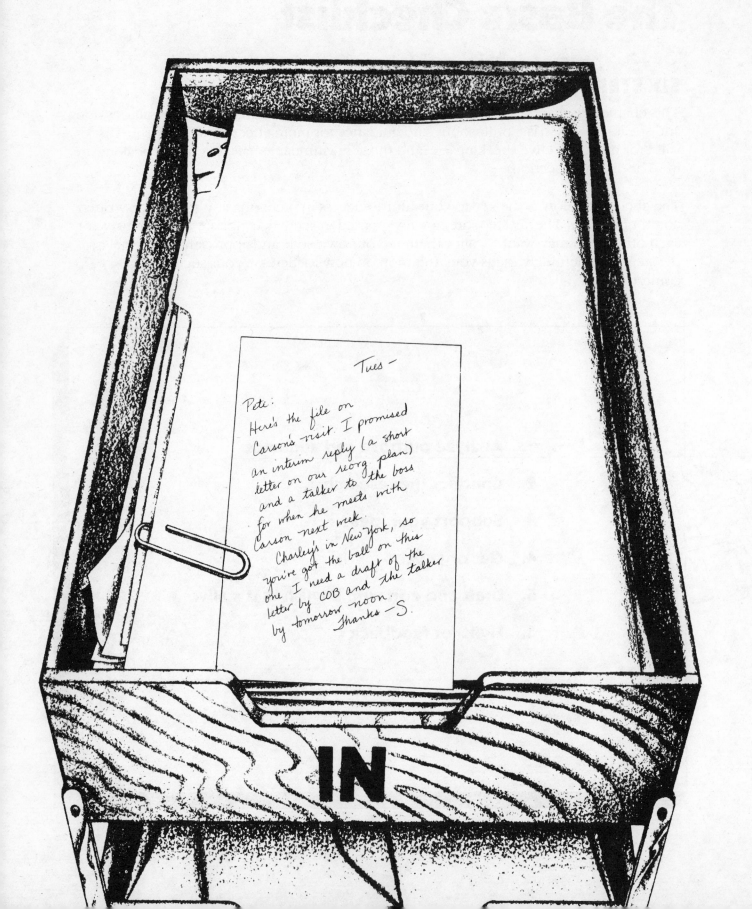

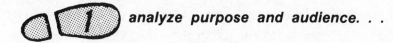 *analyze purpose and audience. . .*

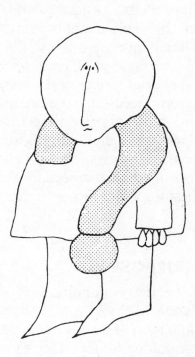

ANALYZE PURPOSE AND AUDIENCE

There it is, smoldering in your in-basket, another chance to excel. . .or rip your knickers. You've done this sort of thing before and realize that the next 30 minutes, more or less, will be used to answer the three questions that should precede any serious attempt at communication:

"Is it necessary?"

"What's my purpose?"

"Who is my audience?"

IS IT REALLY NEEDED?

First, make sure you *need* to communicate. Everyone gripes about the growing pile of paper, but few people ever *do* anything about it. That's got to change if we're to survive the blizzard of correspondence that's already thigh deep. Considering *spoken* communications, how many briefings or presentations do you suppose occur throughout America on a single day? How many committee meetings? The majority of our communications are essential. They could probably be done with less words on fewer pages or in less time with fewer flip charts, but generally speaking, they're necessary. Some portions of our communications, however, are *not* very essential, and some are a complete waste or counterproductive. How about the creation of an eight-page report

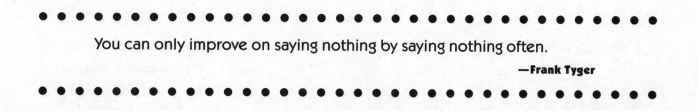

You can only improve on saying nothing by saying nothing often.

—**Frank Tyger**

because the boss said, "I wonder what the impact would be if. . .?" (A phone call or short note reply might have answered the question.) Some executives and staffers are becoming more sensitive to the increasing demands on their shrinking organizations and are questioning some requests for a staff response. In other cases they're responding with much shorter replies or selecting more expedient media such as phone calls rather than letters. An occasional requirement is met by a courageous employee with the comment, "Our top five priority projects are listed; which two should we delay while we work on this project?" Admittedly, those who question staff requests are not part of a large fraternity. However, it's not a closed club, and since resources are almost always scarce, few would deny the need for wider membership. You can certainly challenge every request for a staff response that *you* generate—before you generate it!

MY PURPOSE IS

If the need to communicate *is* necessary, then you're ready to set the process in motion, and your first move is to analyze the purpose. All writing or speaking falls under one or a combination of three general purposes: to direct, to inform (or question), or to persuade. You shouldn't find it difficult to determine the primary purpose your communication must fulfill. Once you decide the purpose, you'll know where to place the emphasis. A directive communication generally emphasizes *what* to do; informative writing or speaking highlights *how*; and persuasion focuses on *why* something should be done. Don't worry about splitting hairs. Almost all of our communications have overlapping purposes; some people even argue that almost everything we say or write is designed to *persuade*—to get someone or some group to *act*—either on a short- or long-term basis. In any case, a few moments spent on thinking about your general purpose will rattle the marbles and prepare you for the important task of identifying your *specific objective*.

What is the "bottom line" in this communication? If you only had one sentence or 30 seconds to explain your specific objective, what would you write or say? If you have a difficult time nailing down your objective, then your audience will be equally confused. If you can't squeeze it into one sentence or phrase, then your target lacks a bull's-eye. One way to get a handle on this is to ask yourself, "What do I want the audience to **do** as a result of my communication?" The answer to that question should be your specific objective. *Don't go any further until you do this!* Once you've done it, you have a lucid,

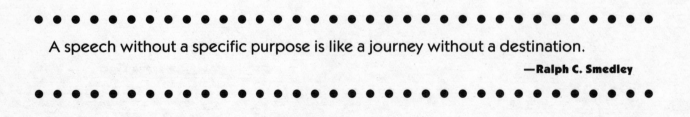

A speech without a specific purpose is like a journey without a destination.

—**Ralph C. Smedley**

concrete objective that will filter, shape, and clarify your efforts. Tack it to the wall or tape it to your desk. Glance at it from time to time as you write and edit. Someone once said, "If you can't write your idea on the back of a business card, you don't *have* an idea!"

THE SENDING AUDIENCE

Every communication has at least two audiences: one at the sending end and one at the receiving end. How can a sender be an audience? Only rarely do we act *unilaterally*. Almost always we speak for our organization or "functional area." Since we speak as staffers, executives, or representatives for our organizations, we must understand the members better and accommodate their views, capabilities, or concerns in our communications. If our communications pertain to established policy, we must fully coordinate. Analyzing an audience at the sending end calls for answers to such questions as these:

Am I promising something my organization can deliver? (You can substitute boss *or* personnel *for* organization.*)*

Is what I'm saying consistent with previous policy or operating philosophy?

Can anyone be embarrassed by what I plan to say or write?

Who needs to coordinate on this? Who else owns a piece of this action?

Does the organization have other objectives that can be skillfully interwoven into this communication although they may not have an immediate bearing on the current issue?

You can follow answers to these general issues with a series of specific questions aimed at individuals—the person who will sign the paper or make the presentation, or the person whom you represent.

What are his or her views on the issue?

What is his or her style? Aloof? Good humored? Subtle? Candid? Deceptive? A risk taker? A don't-rock-the-boater?

How does he or she write or speak? Look at old letters. Check over some of your old drafts that he or she has edited. Check with some of the more perceptive members of the office staff. What reaction do they expect from the signer or presenter?

• •

Every speaker has a mouth; an arrangement rather neat.
Sometimes it's filled with wisdom. Sometimes it's filled with feet.

—Robert Orben

• •

Drawing by N. A. Valencia (by permission)

THE RECEIVING AUDIENCE

When we turn to the audience at the receiving end, we confront an entirely new series of questions:

How do we want them (or him or her) to react to this communication?

Is this audience basically receptive, skeptical, or hostile?

How much do they already know about the subject? What's their background, education, and professional experience?

What tone is appropriate? Warm? Stern?

Is this a message to a CEO or a tech rep? A salesperson or a contractor? What personal information might help you tailor the communication to the individual?

Answers to questions like these pay off. Masters in the art of communications approach audience analysis with what can only be described as *zest*! Figuring every angle and tapping every source of intelligence, they realize that an oversight or misjudgment here could frustrate much of what follows.

LOOKING BACK...

Develop the professional gumption to question some of those communication requirements that crash and burn in your in-basket. If you're up to your axle in work, let your boss know what you intend to shove aside. Perhaps the requirement can be satisfied with a phone call, a short memo, or a routine reply. One aspect of this communications game you directly control is the work you generate for *other* people. If you're a supervisor, sharpen your sensitivity to your people's workloads and limit your requests to essential communications.

Where you stand on an issue often depends on where you sit.

—anonymous

Right now, some people are generating junk mail for you to read or respond to. Clouds of useless presentations enshroud some offices like the aftermath of a mass gas attack. Work multiplies to meet available manpower—and then exceeds even that limit.

It's time we get tough with others and with ourselves. Not everything we author is worthwhile—some of it is trash to attract attention. *Let's knock it off*! And when a load of trivia is dumped on your doorstep, try to reason with the author. Most of us mean well, but we never stop to consider the magnitude of the communications explosion. *Not all of that stuff is worth the time it takes to answer or generate!*

Essential communications, on the other hand, are vital and deserve careful analysis of purpose and specific objective, plus solid detective work on the audiences that sit at both ends. Remember, perceptive analysis of purpose and audience is the first step in putting the reader or listener in your pocket.

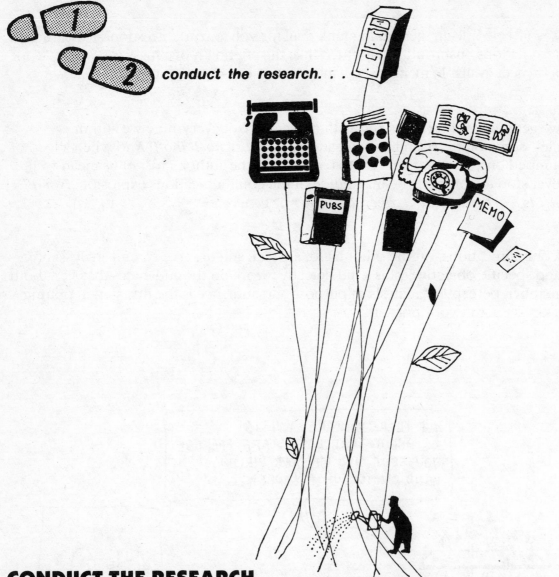

conduct the research. . .

CONDUCT THE RESEARCH

Research seems too simple a word to choke so many people. The word connotes books, raw data, theses, dissertations, annual reports, and market analyses and no doubt implies more frustration than fun. Let's find a better word because most of our research to solve problems is usually not the research we associate with things collegiate or scientific. Does "information retrieval" or "data capture" come closer to hitting the mark? How about *problem solving*? It's literally impossible for anyone to communicate effectively or to do *anything* without spending time digging for data. Every problem, and every communications task you will ever face, begs for a foundation of information—information to which logic is then applied in the search for a solution or response.

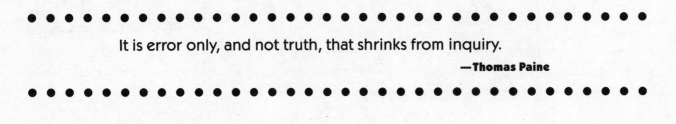

• •

It is error only, and not truth, that shrinks from inquiry.

—**Thomas Paine**

• •

A ROSE BY ANY OTHER NAME

It matters little what we call it as long as we know how to do it—quickly and completely. The objective of all research is either (1) to solve a present or potential problem or (2) to determine if there is a problem. The result of your research can be anything from a short, one-paragraph memo to a comprehensive analysis that weighs out in pounds rather than ounces. The ideas and addresses shown on pages 31 through 35 can aid you in gathering information and support material.

OBJECTIVE AND SCOPE

Spend a few quiet moments just *thinking* about your task. What is your goal? What are the barriers to that goal? Is time limited? Do you have ready access to the necessary sources of information? Try to get some feel for how far you should go in your research, what you can realistically do, and where you should stop. Most staff research tasks are fairly clear in objective and scope. Others are not. When the research task is not clear, you may need to do some preliminary research just to get smart enough to answer the question, "What is (or should be) the objective and scope of this research task?" Do you remember what you read in the previous section about analyzing your purpose and audience?

A RESEARCH PLAN

This plan is nothing more than a series of questions that you jot down about the subject during a public or private brainstorming session. It merely serves as a very loose guide on where to look for info and should keep you in the right mental ballpark when asking questions or analyzing data. Feel free to revise the list of questions as you begin to collect the data and information. On short projects you will probably construct your research plan intuitively and find no need to jot it down.

Never despair, but if you do, work on in despair.

—Burke

YOU AND YOUR ATTITUDE

It's tough to keep an unbiased attitude; in fact, it's probably impossible if you know anything about the subject in question. As you research, you should become aware of your bias. Once you recognize it, you can guard against it. So much for basic outlook; now you're ready to chase after the data.

LOOK IN THE MIRROR

See anything you like? You should be looking a number one resource squarely in the eye. You will be the best source of data for a large part of your work. The primary caution is to be aware of your own biases in working a problem. Don't ignore other data because it's not consistent with your personal philosophy.

FIND IT IN THE FILES—BE THEY PAPER OR DISKS

You probably thought of the office files even before you thought of yourself. Keep a copy of the file plan at your desk and glance at it occasionally. Be aware of files that are being added and files that have been retired. If you have computer files, scan the floppy or hard disk menus. Files are dynamic sources of up-to-date data.

BUDDY, CAN YOU SPARE SOME TIME?

Office mates, secretaries, key supervisors, and folks in other divisions, departments, and offices are likely sources of information. Be specific when you ask, for their time is as valuable as yours.

PUBS, LAWS, AND LETTERS

Regulations, manuals, public laws, policy letters, and operating instructions often represent cornerstones to research. Check your corporate publications file.

Success comes in cans, failure in can'ts.

—Kin Hubbard

DON'T OVERLOOK THE OBVIOUS...

Your organization's history may be a super source for useful data. I say "may" because organization or corporate histories may be nonexistent, or they may have been histories "written by the uninitiated for the disinterested." A good history will contain far more than who died, who got promoted, what got renamed, and which projects were successful; *useful* histories capture the *essence* of important decisions, how problems were solved, what factors were considered, why things *didn't* work like they should have, what anybody *learned* from a particular experience, etc. Quarterly, semiannual, and/or annual financial statements can also be valuable—particularly if you know how to analyze a balance sheet.

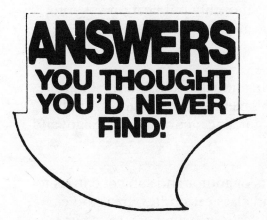

We often waste mountains of time scaling the same peaks someone else already conquered. Valuable data on the issues you investigate, or perhaps even the answers to some of your problems, are available from the following categories of research sources.

PERIODICALS

Check local public, college, and university libraries for the following periodicals if they are not available in your library.

Applied Science and Technology Index —This is a subject index to English-language periodicals in the fields of aeronautics and space science, automation, chemistry, construction, earth sciences, electricity and electronics, engineering, industrial and mechanical arts, materials, mathematics, metallurgy, physics, telecommunication, transportation, and related subjects.

• •

Its name is Public Opinion. It is held in reverence. It settles everything. Some think it is the voice of God.

—Mark Twain

• •

Business Periodicals Index – This is a subject index to English-language periodicals in the fields of accounting, advertising, public relations, automation, banking, communications, economics, finance and investments, insurance, labor management, marketing, taxation, and specific business, industries, and trade.

Congressional Information Service (CIS) Index – CIS collects all the publications of Congress (except the *Congressional Record*). Types of publications include committee hearings, committee prints, House and Senate reports and documents, House and Senate special publications, and Senate executive reports and documents. The CIS Microfiche Library, if available at your library, provides microfiche copies of all publications covered in the CIS Index.

Current Index to Journals in Education (CIJE) – This is a monthly publication covering more than 700 publications. The majority of these publications represent the core periodical literature in the field of education.

Education Index – This is an author/subject index to educational material in the English language. Subject areas include administrative; preschool, elementary, secondary, higher, and adult education; teacher education; counseling and guidance; curriculum design; and curriculum material.

Humanities Index – The main body of the index consists of author and subject entries to periodical articles. Subject fields include archaeology and classical studies, area studies, folklore, history, language and literature, literary and political criticism, performing arts, philosophy, religion, theology, and related subjects.

New York Times Index –This source presents a condensed, indexed history of major world and national events as they were reported each day in the *New York Times*. It includes abstracts of news and editorial matters entered under appropriate headings. Each entry is followed by a precise reference—date, page, and column—to the news story it summarizes.

Public Affairs Information Services Bulletin – This is a weekly bulletin that lists, by subject, current books, pamphlets, periodical articles, government documents, and any other useful library material relating to business, economic, and social conditions, public administration, and international relations.

● ●

He who has no inclination to learn more will be very apt to think that he knows enough.

—**Powell**

● ●

Readers' Guide to Periodical Literature – This is a cumulative author/subject index to periodicals of general interest published in the United States. It covers a broad spectrum of periodicals, including *Aviation Week, Business Week, Congressional Digest, Newsweek, New York Times Magazine, Vital Speeches, Foreign Affairs,* and *World Press Review.*

Government Reports Announcements (GRA) and Index – The Commerce Department's National Technical Information Service (NTIS) is the central point in the United States for public sale of research, development, and other government-funded reports prepared by federal agencies, their contractors, or grantees. GRA abstracts are indexed by subject, personal and corporate authors, and government contract and order numbers. If this index is not available at your library, there is a good possibility that a nearby public or university library will have it.

Ours is the age which is proud of machines that think, and suspicious of men who try to.

—**H. Mumford Jones**

Selected Rand Abstracts – The Rand Corporation is an independent, nonprofit organization engaged in scientific research and analysis. It conducts studies supported by the U.S. government, state and local governments, its own funds, and private sources. Rand is primarily involved with the physical, social, and biological sciences, with emphasis on problems of policy and planning in domestic and foreign affairs.

● ●

> The simple realization that there are other points of view is the beginning of wisdom. Understanding what they are is a great step. The final test is understanding why they are held.
>
> **—Charles M. Campbell**

● ●

ONLINE COMPUTER SERVICES AND SOURCES

The world of computer research is expanding exponentially. There is so much information available to those who have access to a microcomputer and a modem that it would be impossible to catalog the options.

Maxwell Online, Inc., for instance, has two operating divisions: the ORBIT Search Service and BRS Information Technologies. ORBIT offers online access worldwide to over 100 comprehensive databases for scientists and researchers in the fields of chemistry, energy, engineering, materials, and patents. ORBIT's databases include the World Patent Index, Biotechnology Abstracts, Petroleum Abstracts, and INPADOC. BRS, established in 1975, is an online host with over 150 databases covering the medical and physical sciences, social sciences, and business areas. In addition to its traditional online service, BRS offers BRS Colleague, an online service developed specifically for physicians. Important databases offered by BRS include Medline, Embase, BIOSIS, the full-text Comprehensive Core Medical Library, and Psychological Abstracts.

There are, of course, companies that catalog the type of services provided by organizations such as Maxwell Online, Inc. CompuServe Inc., for example, publishes an almanac that contains descriptions of over 400 information service online products. This almanac, available nationwide through retail computer stores, consumer electronic stores, mass merchant stores, and subscription, lists subjects in the following categories: Communication/Bulletin Boards, News/Weather/Sports, Travel/Leisure, The Electronic Mall/Shopping, Money Matters/Markets, Entertainment/Games, Home/Health/Family, Reference/Education, Computers/Technology, Business/Other Interests. Under the listing "Reference/Education," for instance, is an entry that allows the user to access IQuest. IQuest is a fully indexed data file (updated daily) that provides bibliographic as well as full-text documents. Source materials include magazines, newspapers, indexes, conference proceedings, directories, books, newsletters, government documents, dissertations, encyclopedias, patent records, and reference guides!

CompuServe is merely *one* of many companies that provide access to information and data bases at nominal cost. The computer section of your local bookstore has a wealth of sources where you can find listings such as those offered by CompuServe. Once you have several of these information catalogs, you can do your research without leaving your office or den.

I'm lost, but I'm making record time!
—A navy pilot, somewhere over the Pacific, 1944

"*Tonight, we're going to let the statistics speak for themselves.*"

Drawing by Koren; © 1974
The New Yorker Magazine, Inc.

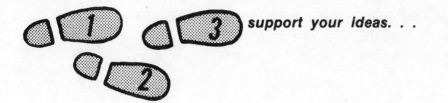 *support your ideas. . .*

WEAK SUPPORT AND FAULTY LOGIC
TRIP UP MORE GOOD WRITERS AND
SPEAKERS THAN ANY OTHER SINGLE
CAUSE...

SUPPORT YOUR IDEAS

The following list contains five potential cures for weak support.

Examples are specific instances chosen to represent or indicate factual data. Good examples must be appropriate, brief, and attention arresting. Quite often they are presented in groups of two or three for impact.

Statistics can be excellent means of support if you handle them competently. Keep them simple and easy to read or understand. One way to do this is to discuss them in terms your audience understands. Also, remember to round off your statistics, whenever possible, and *document* your sources. Saying "Recent studies show that . . ." won't get you anything but cabbage from a smart audience. Tell them the exact source of your statistics.

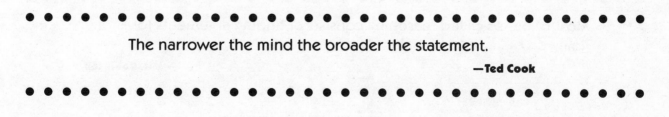

The narrower the mind the broader the statement.

—Ted Cook

Testimony is a means of supporting your opinion with the comments of recognized authorities. These comments can take the form of direct quotes or paraphrases, but direct quotations tend to carry more weight with listeners or readers.

Comparison and **Contrast** are birds of similar feather. Use comparison to dramatize similarities between two objects or situations and contrast to emphasize differences.

Explanation may be used in three ways:

1. *Definition:* a simple explanation in understandable terms of what you're talking about.

2. *Analysis:* division of your subject into small parts, and discussion of the questions who, what, why, where, when, and how.

3. *Description:* similar to "definition" but usually more personal and subjective.

The persuasiveness or believability of your argument or the acceptance of your information depends on the strength of your support material. Keep it simple, relevant, and *accurate!*

Support has a kissin' cousin called logic. When the two of them team up *against* you, you're in trouble. Once we admit that poor support and weak logic can be our problem and not merely the other person's problem, there's hope. It's not possible, or reasonable, to talk about all the logic traps writers and speakers can fall into, but highlighting several of the big ones may keep you on track and avert a future fumble.

YOU BET YOUR BIAS

That's what happens when you gather only the data or opinion that supports your view. This seems too obvious to mention, but sometimes we're not even aware of our blind side. If your bias leads to tunnel vision, you'll never see the counterarguments on the periphery. When you analyze the politics of the situation, you may not want to discuss the opposing viewpoints, but you should recognize them and prepare a counterpunch.

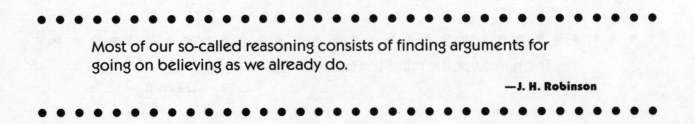

Most of our so-called reasoning consists of finding arguments for going on believing as we already do.

—**J. H. Robinson**

PRESSURE FROM THE THRONE

Sometimes you can't avoid the bias trap. When someone higher than you in the authority chain tries to peddle bias, you may be the hired salesperson. You should *at least* let the boss know that bias, or the possibility of bias, is involved. Good problem solving on your part will expose spongy areas in the argument. Your boss may not be aware of any personal bias, but one of your jobs is to keep him or her out of trouble. If the boss *is* aware and likes it that way, you at least know you're working with the deck stacked against you. Integrity can become an issue in such circumstances.

WILSON'S LAW

In this overmanaged and science-centered world, we find numbers very soothing. Wilson's Law states: "A man with a number is always better off." We are so uncritical of numerical data and so wary of subjective information that we often fall prey to people or papers that spout numbers or statistical proof. Digits are not inherently evil, but excessive reliance on them tends to fog our thinking. Some problems obviously are oriented to numbers, and we can tackle them more effectively from that angle. Other problems are less objective in nature and call for the caution flag when numbers appear. We should remember this useful rule of thumb: Always, *always* examine the basic assumption(s) on which the analysis rests. Some of the most compelling statistical arguments turn out to be intricate sand castles built on foundations of *subjective* assumption. The analysis, in itself, may be defensible, but the assumption(s) can be challenged.

• •

Men are not against you; they are merely for themselves.

—Gene Fowler

• •

LOOPHOLE LOGIC

If you're wise enough to gather adequate support, you may still stumble in the use of it. The following fallacies are samples of slanted reasoning and emotional appeal. Try to keep them out of your work, and learn to identify them in other people's efforts.

Asserted conclusion is an example of drawing conclusions from insufficient data. Any conclusion drawn from weak, sketchy, nonstated, or nonexistent evidence is asserted . . .and not worth a wooden nickel. This is the prime logic fault of writers and speakers. We jump to conclusions from too little evidence; we rely too much on "samples of one" (our own experience); something happens twice the same way, and we assume the ability to *forecast*. The flip side of the asserted conclusion is gullibility. The best defense against an asserted conclusion, if you're on the receiving end, is to ask the other chap to prove it. On the other hand, if you think *you're* in danger of asserting a conclusion, be careful to qualify it. This means introducing your conclusion with a statement like "The trend appears to be. . ." or "Based on these few samples, my *tentative* conclusion is. . . ." Let the reader or listener know that you know the conclusion is weakly supported. Unfortunately, our natural desire is to make positive, solid statements, and this desire encourages the asserted conclusion.

Post hoc fallacy is based on the assumption that because one event follows another, it is necessarily *caused* by the other. One might conclude, for example, that because a higher percentage of executives came up through the initial ranks as a sales representative that sales is the best way to the top. This error in reasoning occurs because we forget, or ignore, other important factors that contribute to the effect. What if the ratio of salespeople to other types of employees was far greater?

Faulty analogy is based on the assumption that what is true of a simple or familiar situation is also true of a complex situation. "Selling a house is as easy as selling a car." Don't you believe it.

Non sequitur fallacy has also been called the old "apples and oranges" argument. Asserting that "Charlie will make a great labor negotiator because he was a first class line foreman" is nonsense. Another common non sequitur in political circles assumes that prowess as a local politician translates into leadership ability at the national or state level. Non sequiturs are conclusions that do not necessarily follow from the facts presented.

● ●

The soundest argument will produce no more conviction in an empty head than the most superficial declamation; a feather and a guinea fall with equal velocity in a vacuum.

—**Colton**

● ●

Hasty generalization results when a few examples used as proof do *not* (or may not) represent the whole. "I asked three of our engineers what they thought of the program, and it's obvious that new product R&D needs an overhaul. . . ."

Faulty dilemma is the implication that no middle ground exists. "We should either fight to win or not get involved." Like it or not, we find a considerable range of options between these two positions.

Stacked evidence is the tendency to withhold facts or manipulate support so that the evidence points in only one direction. Quoting out of context also belongs in this category.

Loaded question, or "begging the question," is the practice of slipping in an assertion and passing it off as a fact. Asking "When are we going to stop sinking money into this expensive program?" asserts a lack of effectiveness in the program but doesn't prove it. Consequently, the implied conclusion is illogical.

● ●

All generalizations are false to a certain extent—including this one.

—Herb Schwartz

● ●

"WELL...YOU REALLY GAVE HIM A PIECE OF YOUR MIND!"

Drawing by N. A. Valencia (by permission)

Another frequent form of begging the question is to assert something and then challenge someone else to disprove it. "How do you know these programs are effective?" puts the listener on the defensive—trying to disprove an implied conclusion. The proper response would be, "How do you know the programs are *not* effective?" Remember, whoever asserts should have the burden of proof. (On the other hand, if the person who asserts is your boss, forget it. The title of this book is not "How to get fired by being logical"!)

Poor compromise. Many problems are satisfactorily solved through compromise, but you should avoid the tendency to accept the compromise solution in all situations. Sometimes it is the *worst* course of action.

Nonexpert opinion or assumed authority. Don't be swayed (or try to sway someone else) based on the opinion of an unqualified authority. The world is chock-full of people who, because of their *position* or authority in *one* field, are quoted on subjects in other fields for which they have limited or no expertise.

Primacy-of-print fallacy. We often laugh at the verbal nonsense of some semiarticulate buffoons, but put their ramblings in *print*, and magically, the comments rise to the level of objective analysis! Be as skeptical and thoughtfully crical of the printed word as you are of the spoken word.

Emotional appeal. Obvious examples of this fallacy range from the use of emotionally charged words to name calling. Some of the less obvious examples include the following:

☞ **Reputation or precedent as sole support.** "AT&T has found the procedure very useful, and we should try it," or "The last three CPAs supported this policy, and that's good enough for me."

☞ **Glittering generality** (or a conclusion wrapped in an attractive label). "Good management principles demand we take this course of action."

☞ **Catch phrases.** "The Crash of '87 proved that program trading must be controlled or reduced; therefore. . . ."

☞ **Bandwagon appeal.** "Every marketing analyst knows that. . . ."

The amount of fallacious reasoning and weak support we see and hear on a daily basis is staggering. We are literally engulfed in mental muck. Indeed, we probably share in the contribution. The challenge is to sharpen our professional sense of smell so we can quickly sniff out the rational from the ridiculous.

The preceding discussion was a review of what to look for in the areas of support and logic when you're running the ball. . .or chasing someone who is. Now that you've analyzed your purpose and audience, conducted the research, and built your logical argument, it's time to organize that material for effective presentation.

• •

We have nothing to fear but fallacy itself.

—H. Schwartz

• •

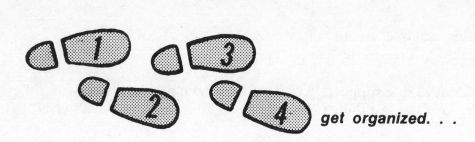

get organized. . .

Just as you tune out a speaker who rambles on without a logical pattern, you stop reading badly organized writing. Few of us are willing to mentally reorganize the material for such a speaker or writer. If you don't organize your material logically and in a sequence that leads your reader from one point to the next, you may as well not write at all. That's why its important to. . .

GET ORGANIZED !

A BASIC FRAMEWORK

Most writing follows a three-part arrangement: introduction, body, and conclusion. This three-part format is so logical you'll probably use it for most of your writing.

There is, of course, more to organization than this simple three-part breakdown. The introduction must capture your reader's attention, establish rapport, and announce your purpose. The body must be an effective sequence of ideas. And, finally, the conclusion must summarize the main points stated in the body and close the whole thing smoothly.

Let's assume you've completed your basic research, and your notes (or assorted letters, reports, etc.) are scattered over the top of your desk—now what? How do you get ready to write?

DETERMINE YOUR BOTTOM LINE

This ought to be easy. It's the same "one liner" you used back there in step one when you were developing your purpose. (In fact, it should still be tacked on the wall or taped to your desk.) It's what you want the audience to do after digesting your communication. Concentrate on it again for a few minutes, and then start with a fresh sheet of paper and . . .

LIST YOUR MAIN AND SUPPORTING IDEAS

If, after looking at your bottom line (statement of purpose), you've exhausted your ideas on your subject (you probably haven't), your task at this point is fairly simple. But, if you have any doubt, continue to jot down any fact or idea that seems to support, or relate to, your purpose statement. The more facts and ideas, the better. When you're reasonably certain that you've completed the list, question each item in the light of your purpose and the needs of your readers. Delete items not directly related to your purpose or not required for reader understanding and acceptance.

Bear in mind that the problem for most writers is too much rather than too little material. If you're like many writers, you may experience some frustration in deciding how much of the material you've gathered is relevant, but relentless questioning will purify the list. Question, sift, revise, and discard until you have only the material you need to support your purpose and the needs of your readers. When you're absolutely certain that you've retained only the relevant material, you're ready to identify main and supporting ideas.

• •

The Carter administration's edict on how to cut costs by writing fewer and shorter government communications was over 50 pages long. Good luck, America.

—**Schwartz**

• •

Main ideas and facts represent major divisions or points you expect to develop in the course of your discussion. When you weigh them against other facts and ideas, they seem to stand out and appear equally important. They are so vital to your purpose that omission of one or the other would leave you with an unbalanced communication. For example, if your purpose is to describe a college recruitment program, your main points might be statements concerning overall funding, target populations, and advertising strategy. Supporting ideas would be descriptive elements that expand each main point in greater detail. The advertising strategy, for example, might describe direct mail, radio, TV, newspaper, and college "open house" campaigns.

Identification of your main and supporting ideas should enable you to establish priorities on the order in which you'll develop your communication. That is, you can determine which point will come first and which will come second, third, and so forth, as you lead your readers step-by-step through your message. This list of main and supporting ideas may be very short if your communication is simple or quite long if you're doing a detailed report.

PICK A PATTERN

Your next step is to select a structure or *pattern* that enables you and your readers to move systematically and logically through your ideas from a beginning to a conclusion. Either your purpose, the needs of your audience, the nature of your material, or a combination of the three will almost always dictate one (or a combination) of the following patterns.

Topical pattern. This is a commonly used pattern to present general statements followed by numbered listings of subtopics to support, explain, or expand the statements. For example, if you make a general statement that students participate in a number of special activities in pursuit of personal interests and hobbies, you could use the topic pattern to list and briefly describe typical activities. In this case, the sequence in which you list the activities would not be important unless you want to begin with the most popular activity and move down the scale to the less popular.

At times, however, the list should follow some logical order, depending on the nature of your material and the purpose of your communication. Some material flows more logically if you arrange it from the simple to the complex, the known to the unknown, the general to the specific, the specific to the general, and so on. The best approach in using this pattern is to experiment with the arrangements that will best help your readers understand what you're saying.

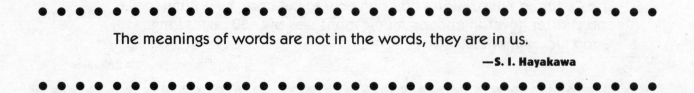

The meanings of words are not in the words, they are in us.

—S. I. Hayakawa

PICKING
PROPER
PATTERNS
PORTENDS
PALPABLY
POTENT
PRODUCTS,
PARAGON
PENMEN,
PROUD
PUBLICISTS,
    and
PAROXYSMS of PUBLIC PLEASURE

— WING WANG WOO
CONFUSE-US COOKIE CO.

Time or chronological pattern. When you use this pattern, you discuss events, problems, or processes in the sequence of time in which they take place or should take place (past to present, present to past, or present to future). This pattern is the simplest and most commonly used approach in writing because you so frequently encounter situations based on time sequences. Of course, you must be careful to select facts that support the purpose of your communication. In most cases, this pattern is used in writing histories, tracing the evolution of processes, recording problem conditions and solutions, and dealing with other situations that develop over extended periods.

Reason pattern. You can use this pattern if you want to state an opinion or point of view and then develop support by discussing reasons. For example, in discussing a problem with the boss, you might express an opinion or point of view that, you think, would lead to a solution. The boss might ask you to put the opinion in writing and discuss the logic that led to the opinion. Your approach might be to write a complete statement of the opinion or point of view and then discuss each reason for the idea in a series of numbered paragraphs.

Problem-solution pattern. You can use this pattern to identify and describe a problem or issue and then discuss possible solutions to the problem or techniques for resolving an issue. This pattern may be used in several variations.

One variation is to present a complete description of a problem and then discuss what you perceive as the single, most logical solution. Of course, you'll want to discuss all facets of the problem—its origin, its characteristics and impact, and any consequences. And, in your proposed solution, you'll need to include enough factual information to convince your readers that the solution is practical and cost effective. As part of your discussion, you might explain how to implement the solution. Another variation is to offer several possible solutions, show the effect of each solution, and then discuss what you consider as the best alternative.

Another variation is to use the pro-and-con approach to discuss a problem and possible solutions. You'll find this pattern useful when you're for or against someone else's proposal, or when you're considering alternate solutions offered by several other people. One technique in using this variation is to begin with a description of the problem and the alternate solutions. You then analyze and question the strengths and weaknesses of the proposed solutions. You conclude by discussing your solution to the problem and showing how your proposals are superior. This is not a format for a personal attack on an adversary; it's simply a systematic approach to use in persuading people either to accept your ideas or to modify their own ideas.

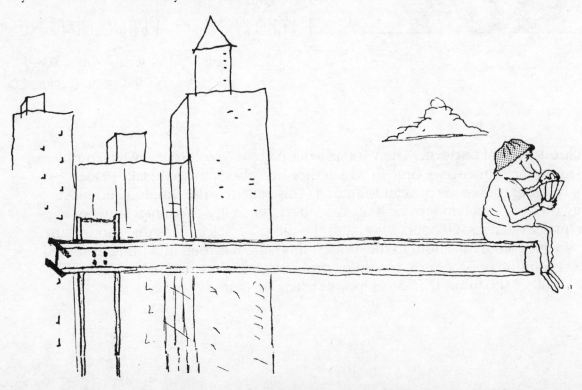

Spatial or geographical pattern. When you use this pattern, you'll start at some point in space and proceed in sequence to other points. The pattern is based on a directional strategy—north to south, east to west, bottom to top, above and below, clockwise or counterclockwise, etc. For example, you might describe an auto assembly line from start to finish, the services offered by a library on the first floor, second floor, and the third floor, or the view from one point in a clockwise or counterclockwise movement through space to another point.

One caution: Make sure to use appropriate transitions to indicate spatial relationships—to the left, farther to the left, still farther to the left; adjacent to, a short distance away, etc. Otherwise you can easily confuse or disorient your readers.

Cause-and-effect pattern. You can use a cause-and-effect pattern to show how one or more ideas, actions, or conditions lead to other ideas, actions, or conditions. Two variations of this pattern are possible: cause to effect and effect to cause. To use the cause/effect variation, you might begin by identifying ideas, actions, or conditions and then show how they have produced or will produce certain effects. For example, in discussing increased numbers of women in the workplace, you might first describe how a two-income family has almost become a necessity. One effect of this reality might be that women are approaching parity with men in wages/salaries—up from 50 to 70 percent in the past decade.

You can also use an effect/cause approach with the same example by reversing the conditions. You could begin by discussing increases in women's wages/salaries (the effect) and argue that more women in the work force are responsible (the cause). The technique you use depends on the context of your discussion.

N. A. Valencia (by permission)

Whichever strategy you use, avoid false causes and single causes. You're guilty of using a false cause when you assume that one event or circumstance causes a second event or circumstance merely because it precedes the second event or circumstance. Many people observe that circumstance B occurred after circumstance A and conclude that A caused B. The conclusion is based on false cause. And you're guilty of using a single cause when you assume that one condition is responsible for a series of conditions. For example, in the illustration above, the real cause of increasing parity in wages may be a series of successful court cases against employers.

Many times your material will dictate the pattern you use; but, unless the pattern is suited to your purpose and audience, don't hesitate to try another one. Try to choose a pattern that permits you to move from the familiar to the unfamiliar or from the simple to the complex.

After you've decided on a specific subject heading, identified your main and supporting points, and selected an appropriate organizational pattern, your next step is to outline your material in the framework as it will appear in your letter, message, report, presentation, etc.

ARRANGE IDEAS IN OUTLINE FORM

You may be one of those exceptional writers who needs no outline; your ideas flow naturally from the beginning of your message or report to the end. But, if you're a typical writer, some kind of blueprint can serve as a time-saver rather than a time-waster.

If you plan to write a short letter, message, or report, your list of main points may be all you need. Even so, you'll find it helpful to arrange them according to their order of importance. Which idea or ideas will you use in the main part of your discussion? Which will you use at the end? As a minimum, jot down your main points in some kind of orderly arrangement before you begin to write.

• •

Let's get rid of the thought that there's nothing to communications.
Let's recognize that communications is tough, hard, demanding.
It's one of the most damned and least understood skills in existence.
It's at the core of every problem facing us as individuals, families, groups, nations.

—**Roy G. Foltz**
"Management by Communication"
Chilton Publishing, 1973

• •

For longer papers, reports, staff studies, and the like, you'll find a detailed outline is usually an indispensable aid in organizing your material. Even though developing the outline can be a laborious process, it forces you to align your main and supporting ideas in logical order before you begin writing. Otherwise, distractions of all kinds can muddle your mind and make your writing job much more difficult than it should be.

It's not necessary to be overly concerned with form in outlining. Use any form that works! Although most writing texts lay out elaborate formats for topic and sentence outlines, *your purpose in outlining is to arrange main and supporting ideas in a visible framework that permits you to see and test your logic on paper.* Then, if some ideas don't fit together or flow naturally, you can rearrange them before you get under way with your big job. There are no absolutes for organizing; everyone has a different mental approach to the task.

"Phone for you, Al."

Drawing by Stevenson; © 1963
The New Yorker Magazine, Inc.

REMEMBER...

Organize before you write. Whether you're experienced enough to organize your material mentally or, like most of us, use pencil and paper—*organize*. Then, and *only* then, should you begin to think about writing that first draft.

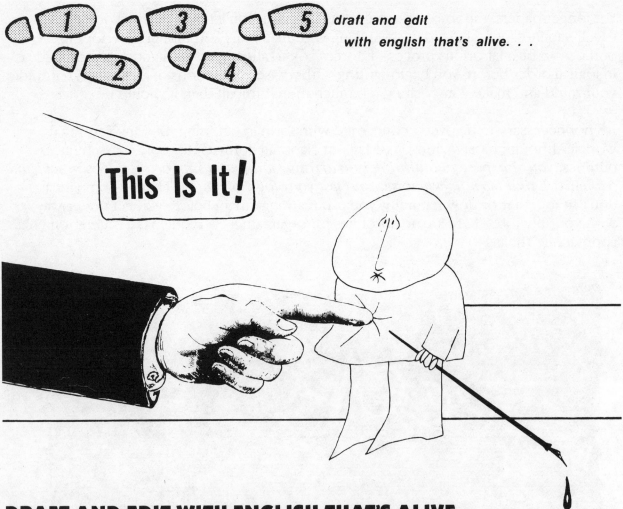

draft and edit
with english that's alive. . .

This Is It!

DRAFT AND EDIT WITH ENGLISH THAT'S ALIVE

Actually, this fifth step is a *shuffle* because there are three separate but closely related mini-steps involved. The first mini-step is learning how to develop effective sentences and paragraphs—and doing it with English that's alive. The second mini-step is learning how to overcome the "first-draft syndrome." Finally, you'll need to develop a thorough and effective system for editing your work (and the work of others). At this point you may be asking yourself, "Why combine three steps into one?" Because you'll actually be doing all three mini-steps at once. Drafting and editing with English that really *communicates* need a *synthesis* of the various skills just mentioned; but since no one can talk or write about three things at once, we'll cover this fifth step in three little pieces. And the first piece is a quick refresher course on how to build decent sentences and paragraphs with English that's alive. Ready?

BUILDING BETTER SENTENCES...

Just think about the horrible writing (or boring speeches) you've been subjected to over the years. Why is it so many of us feel our writing must be dull and lifeless to sound official? Substitute the word "pompous" for "official" and you get the point. Pompous, bureaucratic writing is *garbage*. And like garbage, it should be thrown out!

IS YOUR ACTIVE VOICE ALL BOTTLED UP?

Most of the garbage is created by those who write in the passive voice. If that's you, then you can give yourself mouth-to-mouth resuscitation by simply *activating the passive voice.* Why do we often write in smothered verbs when we seldom *talk* passively? Poor example and bad habit, no doubt. Writing in the passive voice is a disease. The only way to immunize yourself is to recognize the passive voice and keep most of it out of your writing. You'll find that sentences in easy-to-read books, magazines, and letters are about 75 percent active and 25 percent passive voice. Bureaucratic writers usually reverse that ratio! Sentences written in the passive voice lack vitality and sound as though they were written by some gray and anonymous "they."

> Your support is appreciated. . . .
>
> Orders should be submitted. . . .
>
> The ad hoc committee will be appointed. . . .

Yawn. The *actor* in the sentence is either obscure, absent altogether, or just lying there. Who appreciates? Who should order? Who appoints? Why not write. . .

> I appreciate your support. . . .
>
> You should order. . . .
>
> Marion Hargrove will appoint the ad hoc. . . .

The writer steps out of the shadows. Not only does the *actor* get a shot of adrenalin, but the verbs come alive as well. You don't have to be a grammarian to identify the passive voice. Simply write (or rewrite) the majority of your sentences to stress *actor*, *action*, and then *all else*:

> **The President must activate. . . .**
>   (actor)   (action)   (all else)

When we overuse the passive voice and reverse the natural subject-verb-object pattern, our writing becomes lifeless. The active voice makes us human. Our sentences reach out to the reader, and we can get to the point directly with active verbs and fewer words. Bust that bottle and work in the fresh air!

• •

The proliferation of volatile configurations of the model 40 does not lend itself to interchangeability of substitution.

—on a Pentagon bulletin board for all to mock

• •

JUDGE THE JARGON; DUMP THE GOOK

The aim of all communication is to make a personal contact in the simplest possible way, and the simplest way is to use familiar, everyday words. Above all, it must be adapted to specific circumstances (a minimum of jargon) and be devoid of gobbledygook. Jargon consists of "shorthand" words, phrases, or abbreviations that are peculiar to a relatively small group of people. "Debt service," "A.R.M.," "401K," "golden parachute," "CRT," and "VCR" are samples of jargon. When you use jargon *make sure you have carefully assessed the audience*! Will they all understand what you're saying or writing? Gobbledygook, on the other hand, *never* serves a useful purpose. It's merely mumbo-jumbo jibberish used to fill space and impress the innocent. You see a lot of it in reports, military budget requests, congressional testimony, broker's financial forecasts, music and art reviews, and academic texts in the social sciences, arts, and humanities. Turn to page 226 for laughable examples.

"You can even name your own quid pro quo."

© 1975 Al Ross and *Saturday Review*

THE TONE AT THE TIME WILL BE...

Tone is also an important aspect of communication. A dignified tone, a polite tone, an understanding tone—all must be cultivated. Any unintentional manifestation of irritability, brusqueness, or superiority is certain to reduce or destroy your effectiveness. The key is to be aware of your tone and use it appropriately.

STEER CLEAR OF TRITE OR OVERUSED WORDS AND PHRASES

"State-of-the-art," "interface," "quantity," and the ever-popular "in order that" are words and phrases (like hundreds of others) that move in and out of vogue. Avoid the temptation to become a slave to current fashion. Although many of these words and phrases may be appropriate when used in a specific context, their use has proliferated far beyond the parameters of the various ramifications of their original connotations, vis-à-vis . . .

UNNECESSARY WORDS

Many writers and speakers add unnecessary words to their phrases because they think padding emphasizes or rounds out a passage. For example, they frequently write "final completion," "month of January," or "close proximity." The completion must be final, or it is not complete; January must be a month; proximity *means* close. Here is a list of some padded phrases frequently used in communications. The underscored words are unnecessary.

It came <u>at a time</u> when. . . .

During <u>the year of</u> 1968. . . .

. . .at a meeting <u>held</u> in Washington.

We will ascertain the facts <u>at a</u> later <u>date</u>.

In about two weeks' <u>time</u>. . . .

In <u>the city of</u> Valdosta, Georgia. . . .

The targets are made <u>out</u> of alumite.

During the <u>course of the</u> trip. . . .

Perhaps <u>it may be that</u> Crocksmyer is reluctant. . . .

At this point <u>in time</u>. . . .

• •

A writer is in the broadest sense a spokesman of his community. Through him that community comes to know its heart. Without such knowledge, how long can it survive?

—Saul Bellow

• •

BIG WORDS VERSUS LITTLE WORDS

Some folks feel a large vocabulary of big words marks them as learned; but, most of the time, short words do a better job. This does not mean a large vocabulary is not an asset. On the contrary, the more words a writer has to call upon, the more clearly and forcibly he or she can communicate. But why use "ultimate" when you mean "final," or "prerogative" when you mean "privilege," or "transpire" when you mean "occur"?

VARIOUS SHADES OF MEANING

Use different words to express various shades of meaning. This is the reason a large vocabulary is helpful. The writer with an adequate vocabulary writes about the *aroma* of a cigar, the *fragrance* of a flower, the *scent* of perfume, or the *odor* of gas instead of the *smell* of all of these things. There is a reason for using words of more than one syllable.

SENTENCE LENGTH

Since the purpose of correspondence is to transfer a thought to the reader in the simplest manner with the greatest clarity, you should avoid long, complicated sentences. Break up long, stuffy sentences by making short sentences of dependent clauses. Short sentences increase the pace; long ones usually retard it. The key is to vary your pattern. Constant use of either form can become monotonous.

WORDS THAT ANTAGONIZE

Words that carry uncomplimentary insinuations, make negative suggestions, or call up unpleasant thoughts are tactless, and they frequently defeat your purpose. Be aware that some expressions may humiliate or belittle the folks you are communicating with.

© 1975 Hal Hancock and *Saturday Review*

"THAT" AND "WHICH"

In a condensed article for *Reader's Digest* from "Say What You Mean," author Rudolf Flesch suggests the following:

> Leave out the word "that" whenever possible. *You can often omit it without changing the meaning at all. Take this sentence: "We suggest that you send us your passbook once a year." Now strike out* that. *Isn't this better and smoother? Again, this is something we do all the time in speaking.*
>
> *And while you're crossing out* that's, *also go on a* which *hunt. For some reason people think* which *is a more elegant pronoun. Wrong. Usually you can replace* which *by* that, *or leave it out altogether—and you'll get a better, more fluent, more "spoken" sentence.*

POSITIVE APPROACH

Use a positive approach. The following example shows that a positive approach is much more forceful than a negative approach:

Negative: We cannot pay you in full before August 8.

Positive: We will pay you in full on or shortly after August 8.

Well, so much for breathing a little life into that stale English we so often read and write. Now it's time to put that resuscitated English to work—in paragraphs.

PARAGRAPHING...AND THE "ONE-RIDER-PER-HORSE" PRINCIPLE

Paragraphs are the primary vehicles for developing your ideas, and they serve three important purposes:

- To group related ideas into single units of thought.
- To separate one unit of thought from another unit.
- To alert your readers you're shifting to another phase of your subject.

Every paragraph you write should fulfill this threefold purpose. In general, paragraph development follows the organizational pattern you selected in step four. That is, you build your paragraphs to meet the structural requirements of your overall communication. But you can use analogy, examples, definition, and comparison and contrasts to develop single paragraphs within your overall pattern. The guiding principle is to develop *one main idea in each paragraph*. One rider per horse!

Most corporate communication depends on relatively short paragraphs of four to seven sentences. Unfortunately, paragraph length tends to be longest in the academic and governmental sectors of America. Perhaps this is due to the "publish or perish" philosophy on campus and the penchant for obfuscation in politics. If you follow the corporate practice, you'll be more likely to develop clear, easy-to-read paragraphs. This doesn't mean that **all** your paragraphs should be the same length—that would be monotonous and may reflect inadequate development.

Too many writers consider paragraphing an arbitrary task; that is, they create a paragraph anytime they feel like it. At some point, they say, "Well, it's about time for a paragraph." Don't do that!

An effective paragraph is a functional unit with clusters of ideas built around a *single main idea* and linked with other clusters preceding and following it. It's not an arbitrary collection designed for physical convenience. It must perform a definite, planned function —present a single major idea or point, describe an event, create an impression, etc. Clusters of ideas in a true paragraph must convey a nucleus of meaning closely related to the meaning that runs through other clusters of ideas. It can perform this function only if it contains a family of sentences that contribute to its main idea.

TOPIC SENTENCES…SIGNPOSTS IN THE JUNGLE

The most important sentence in any paragraph you write is the **topic sentence**. Why? It expresses the main idea of your paragraph and gives you a point of focus for supporting details, facts, figures, and examples. And it prepares your readers for your supporting information. In short, the topic sentence is the subject or controlling idea of the paragraph, and it signals the kind of information needed to support it.

Since the topic sentence is the subject and main idea of the paragraph, it's **normally** the first sentence in the paragraph. Other sentences between the topic sentence and the last sentence must be closely related to the topic sentence in the sense they document, expand, emphasize, and support the topic sentence. The last sentence should either summarize points made about the topic sentence, clinch the main idea in the reader's mind, or serve as a transition to the next topic sentence. You should omit any sentence that doesn't perform one of these functions!

● ●

If you don't know the word—you can't think the thought.

—B. Meuse

● ●

Practice in developing paragraphs according to this arrangement will not only assure you of tightly organized paragraphs, it'll also enable you to offer a convenience to your readers. Many people need only general information about the content of certain letters, reports, and directives. For these people, the convenience of scanning topic sentences at the beginning of paragraphs for the most important ideas can save valuable time. And, if they need more details, they can always read beyond your topic sentences.

When you write more than one paragraph in a communication, make sure your sentences and paragraphs flow smoothly into each other. Use of clear-cut topic sentences followed by supporting and clinching sentences is an important step in that direction. But you can develop your paragraphs according to this pattern and still produce jerky writing. Your objective is to help your readers see your paragraphs as integrated units rather than mere collections of sentences.

THE BULLETIN BOARD

TO CONTRAST IDEAS

but
yet
nevertheless
however
still
conversely
on the one hand
instead of
neither of these
(to) (on) the
    contrary
rather than
no matter what
much less as
in contrast
otherwise
on the other hand
in the (first)
    (second) place
nor
according to

TO SHOW TIME

immediately
presently
nearly a . . . later
meantime
meanwhile
afterward
next
as of today
this year, however,
a little later
then
last year
next week
tomorrow
as of now
finally

TO RELATE THOUGHTS

indeed
anyway, anyhow
elsewhere
nearby
above all
even these
beyond
in other words
for instance
of course
in short
in sum
yet
in reality
that is
by consequence
notwithstanding
nonetheless
as a general rule
understandably
traditionally
the reason, of course
the lesson here is
from all information
at best
naturally
in the broader sense
to this end
in fact

TO COMPARE IDEAS

like
just as
similar
this

TO SHOW RESULTS

therefore
as a result
thus
consequently
hence

TO ADD IDEAS

first, second, next, last, etc.
in addition
additionally
moreover
furthermore
another
besides
clear, too, is
the answer does not only lie
to all that
more than anything else
here are some. . . facts
now, of course, there are
now, however
what's more
also

One way to improve the flow of your ideas is to *think in paragraphs* rather than sentences. Once you develop a topic sentence (the main idea), think of the points you need to expand, clarify, illustrate, and explain the implications of that sentence. How many supporting points are necessary, and how can you best tie the points together in a final sentence? Think ahead through the logic you plan to develop, and then frame your sentences accordingly. If you think in terms of one sentence at a time, you must begin a new thought process when you get ready to write the second sentence. The process takes you through a series of stops and starts, and your writing is likely to reflect that jerkiness in your reader's mind. They may also have the same problem in moving from paragraph to paragraph. The key to smooth movement between ideas, of course, is to climb aboard the. . .

RAPID TRANSIT

On the facing page you'll find a variety of words and phrases that can be used to help your reader move from idea to idea as your communication unfolds. These *transitional devices* provide the ideal logic links between your key points and the mind of the reader. Take a look at the bulletin board. . . .

Woven skillfully into your writing, these devices will make it easier for your readers to follow your line of thought. Use of pronouns that refer to nouns in preceding sentences, repetitions of key words and ideas, and use of connecting words and phrases are also a few ways to bridge gaps in thought and move readers from one idea to another.

Rather than use the same nouns in sentence after sentence, substitute pronouns in some sentences to refer back to the nouns. For example, such pronouns as "he," "she," "it," "this," "these," "those," and "they" can refer to people, words, or ideas in a preceding sentence or paragraph. They can be very effective transitions, but they require definite antecedents. What about the use of "they" in the preceding sentence?

Another kind of transition is to repeat key words and ideas. Notice how the writer of the following paragraph repeated "simplicity," "incisiveness," and "focus" to make points clear:

> *Effective presentation of concepts depends on <u>simplicity</u>, <u>incisiveness</u>, and <u>focus</u>. <u>Simplicity</u> is necessary because time constraints preclude elaboration and detailed discussion of complicated relationships. <u>Incisiveness</u> fixes an idea in the listener's mind. An <u>incisive</u> presentation appeals to common sense and facilitates understanding. <u>Focus</u> strips ideas to their essentials and promotes the presenter's objectives. A presentation is <u>focused</u> when it deals with a limited subject.*

A number of words and phrases function as transitional connectives. You'll commonly use these words and phrases at or near the beginning of your sentences to signal a relationship between one sentence and a preceding sentence. For example (a transitional

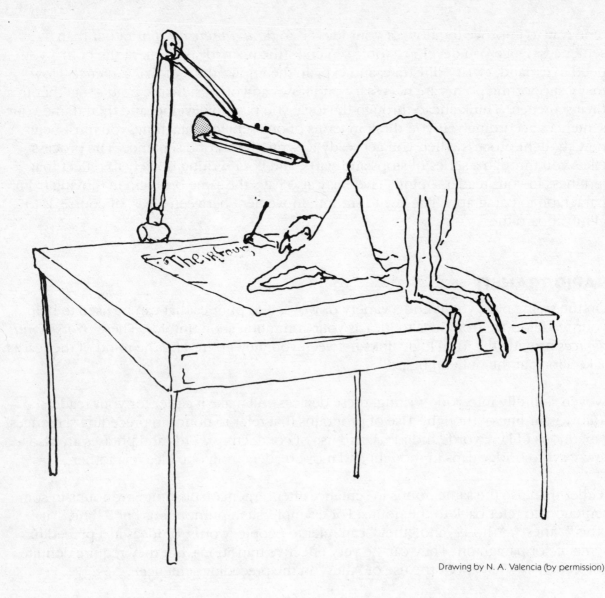

Drawing by N. A. Valencia (by permission)

phrase signaling illustration), such words as "finally," "next," "therefore," "however," and "furthermore" establish relationships based on time, position, conclusion, contrast, and addition. Notice the role of "however" in this next example:

In past tests, only one person in five was able to complete Part I in less than two hours. During the last examination period, <u>however</u>, three of every five people completed it within one hour.

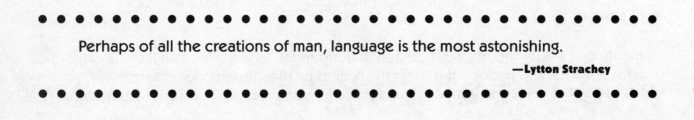

Perhaps of all the creations of man, language is the most astonishing.

—**Lytton Strachey**

A gap in meaning separates the two ideas: the writer is comparing the abilities of two different groups of people. "However" signals the reader to a contrasting relationship between two major ideas. You also can use such phrases as "in addition to," "on the other hand," "in other words," "toward this objective," and "in the meantime" to show specific relationships.

Certain kinds of clauses can function as transitions to show relationships of time ("after you complete that process"), result ("since we have this problem"), and concession ("although that condition persists"). Technically, these clauses function as adverbs. This means you use them only as they relate properly to the main verbs in your sentences.

Transitional sentences and paragraphs can also be used, although they are usually reserved for longer communications. (That sentence made a transitional paragraph that moved you from discussion of words, phrases, and clauses to discussion of sentences and paragraphs.)

When you use a transitional sentence, you'll normally use it at the end of a paragraph. It'll actually serve two purposes: signal the end of the paragraph and lead the reader to the main or topic idea of the next paragraph. But a transitional sentence can be the first sentence of a paragraph. It'll also serve two purposes: topic sentence of the paragraph, and transition between what follows it and the preceding paragraph. Here's an example of a transitional sentence that could come at the end or beginning of a paragraph.

> *Fortunately, we can solve these parking problems if we offer our people some incentives to use car pools.*

If the sentence is the last sentence of a paragraph, the paragraph would offer a solution to the problems. The topic sentences of the next paragraph might be written like this:

> *At least three incentives could be used: preferred parking spaces, guaranteed working hours, and distant parking for nonparticipants.*

But, if the first paragraph ends with a sentence dealing with the seriousness of problems, our sentence beginning with "fortunately" could serve as a topic sentence of the second paragraph. Again, transitional sentences are usually more appropriate for longer communications. Words, phrases, and clauses are more appropriate for letters, messages, memos, and other relatively short writing formats.

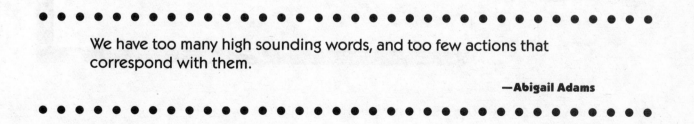

We have too many high sounding words, and too few actions that correspond with them.

—Abigail Adams

Transitional *paragraphs* are usually reserved for long papers and reports that contain major sections or chapters. A transitional paragraph may be used to summarize one section and lead the reader to the next section. Or it may introduce the next section and tie it to the preceding section.

There's nothing new or mysterious about the writing techniques discussed so far. We know they work because they've proven themselves in all kinds of writing situations. If there's any formula for effective writing, it's planning, organizing, and applying these time-tested principles. But, like any other task, writing is not limited to a single set of rules or steps. You may have a proven formula of your own, or you may want to modify these techniques to suit your purpose, your boss, your readers, or an established corporate, governmental, military, or academic format.

Whatever your approach, however, you'll eventually have to write that first draft. Are you ready for mini-step number two?

FIRST-DRAFT SYNDROME

Writers come in two sizes: those who intuitively "wing" a first draft without an outline, and those who work from a written plan. Either way, they both face the "first-draft syndrome." This syndrome can be recognized by any one or all of the following symptoms:

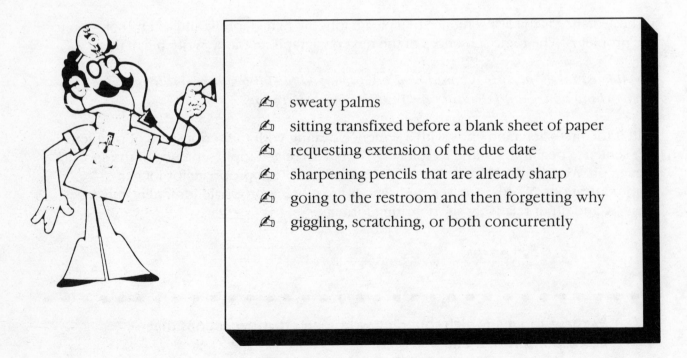

- ✍ sweaty palms
- ✍ sitting transfixed before a blank sheet of paper
- ✍ requesting extension of the due date
- ✍ sharpening pencils that are already sharp
- ✍ going to the restroom and then forgetting why
- ✍ giggling, scratching, or both concurrently

The best advice on how to get started with the first draft is to. . .

To establish the appropriate framework for your communication, select the proper format from the *Tongue* or *Quill* section of this book. Look closely at the introductions, bodies, and conclusions used in these examples, and then form your material in a similar format. (If your corporation, agency, or department uses modifications of these formats, follow the local guidance.)

PUTTING YOUR LAST LINE FIRST

As you begin your first draft, *put your last line first* (and don't be surprised if it looks similar to your original statement of purpose). Much of our correspondence reads like a Mary Roberts Reinhart mystery—plot twists, blind alleys, and partial explanations. We're held in suspense until the last paragraph. That approach made money for the queen of mystery, but is a murderous waste of time for writers, readers, speakers, and listeners! Lieutenant Colonel Tom Murawski, former Director of Executive Writing at the U.S. Air Force Academy and co-developer of the USAF's Effective Writing Course, explains:

> *Our recommended approach to organized writing inverts the normal inductive thinking pattern; we ask writers to begin where their thinking ends up. Though this pattern may seem to put the cart before the horse, it is really nothing more than the newspaper technique of placing the heart of a story early. The advantage of spilling the beans is that it saves wear and tear on a reader's patience, for it reveals right away what any details add up to.*

To make the bottom line your top line, simply open with your main point. When responding to someone, start with what concerns that someone the most. When writing on your own, start with what concerns you most. Answer questions and then explain them. Make requests and then justify them. Give conclusions and then support them. Imagine you're talking to your reader on the phone and expect to get cut off any moment. What would you say? *That's* your main point!

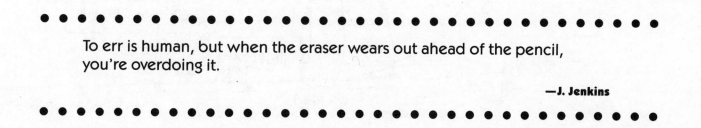

To err is human, but when the eraser wears out ahead of the pencil, you're overdoing it.

—J. Jenkins

Delay your main point only if it will make no sense without introductory details or if you want to soften criticism by starting with something positive. But, in either case, don't leave your reader in suspense. Just as people dislike a speaker who takes forever to get to the point, they also dislike the writer who isn't "up front."

Poorly organized letters often start with something painfully obvious like, "We received your January 16 request." Then clue-by-clue the letter unfolds details that make sense only toward the end. There, just after a signal like "therefore" or "due to the above," all is revealed. This pattern of building to the main point isn't chaotic, but neither is it efficient. An efficient letter reads like a newspaper article or newscast. It starts with the heart of a story and then elaborates.

For you, the writer, this news article approach provides a reliable way to overcome the tyranny of the blank page. You needn't search for something—anything—to get yourself started. By coming to your point right away, you can easily check the relevance of whatever you might add. You won't be able to write "We received your January 16 request" after you've opened your letter with a specific reply.

For your readers, the news article approach makes your writing clear the first time through. They don't have to read your work twice: first to see where the preliminaries are headed and then to study those preliminaries in context.

Having written your last line first, you're ready to follow the simple road signs of introduction, body, and conclusion.

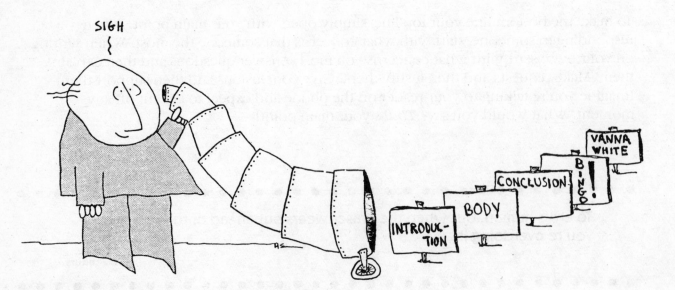

"...AND I WOULD LIKE TO THANK YOU ALL FOR ENDURING THIS BRIEF INTRODUCTION, NOW... LET ME SAY..."

Drawing by N. A. Valencia (by permission)

THE INTRODUCTION

The introduction orients your readers to the content of your communication. It sets the stage and provides clues to your message. Although the content and length of your introduction may vary with your purpose, it should always be brief and pointed. At the absolute minimum, your introduction is that bottom line we talked about a few paragraphs back. In fact, a simple one-sentence statement of your purpose will be appropriate for many of your writing situations.

How about this one? "I regret I can't attend your January conference because I have a prior commitment." An introduction like this isn't elegant, but it gets right to the point. It tells your readers exactly what they need to know: you can't attend the conference. You could probably soften the blow a bit if you add ". . . thanks for the invitation," but it's not necessary. The statement of regret is adequate. If you feel it's necessary, you can explain your regret or comment on the conference in other paragraphs.

Use the same technique in other situations: give directives *before* reasons, requests *before* justifications, answers *before* questions, etc. In other words, get to your main point as soon as possible without bruising sensitivities, muddying minds, or dispatching your audience to "never-never land."

● ●

My interest is in the future because I'm going to spend the rest of my life there.

—**Charles F. Kettering**

● ●

Another introduction to a short communication might read like this:

> *The long-range product development group makes a critical contribution to our corporate mission. This letter outlines your responsibilities as a new member of this group. You have certain specific responsibilities during the budget development cycle, engineering forecast meetings, and market analysis tasking sessions.*

The first sentence is a simple stage-setting remark that helps focus the reader's attention on the subject of the letter. The second sentence is a clear statement of purpose: to inform the reader of new responsibilities. The third sentence provides an overview of three main points covered in the body.

Another point to remember: even though the introduction is the first part of a communication readers see, you don't have to write it first. If the introduction doesn't come easily or naturally, you can work on another part of the communication and return later to the introduction. Some writers delay work on the introduction until the rest of the communication is written. Others insist that the introduction guides them in shaping the content/body of their message.

THE BODY SHOP

The *body* of your communication is the message you convey in support of your purpose. It includes your main ideas about your subject and supporting details under each main idea necessary to explain and clarify your purpose. The more main ideas you have to develop, the more supporting details are necessary to accomplish your purpose. You know from our previous discussion that in a relatively short letter, you'll probably have a separate paragraph for each of your main ideas, but you should *never* try to develop two or more main ideas in a single paragraph. (In a longer communication, you may find it necessary to use *more* than one paragraph or subparagraph to cover one main idea.)

If you're working from an outline of your information, it'll indicate your main ideas and supporting details for each idea. All you need to do now is to glance occasionally at the outline so that you say what is necessary to accomplish your purpose. But don't allow an outline to slow you down. Your primary purpose at this point is to *get your ideas on paper.* You need to write while the ideas come easily. Don't stop to revise your statements, and don't worry about the way you express yourself. You can revise and polish your writing *after* you develop a rough draft.

DETAIL... HOW MUCH IS TOO MUCH?

Another principle in developing your first draft is to make sure you include enough explanation and detail for your readers to understand what you're talking about. Writers too often assume incorrectly that readers have background information and complete knowledge of a subject. Remember that your communication should be complete enough to stand on its own. Your readers should know exactly what you're talking about and what you expect of them when they read your correspondence, messages, reports, and other papers.

• •

I have never been lost. I was mightily confused for three days once—but never lost!

—R.M. Doucet, Lt. Col. USAF (Ret.)
Master Navigator, B-52s

• •

Thus, in developing your first draft, *don't worry about including too much detail*. When you revise and edit the draft, you can combine main and supporting ideas, delete excess material, and otherwise improve the movement of your logic from idea to idea. It's far better to have too many ideas than too few. You can always delete excess material more easily than you can add new material.

One other suggestion: whether you dictate, write in longhand, use a typewriter, or hammer your first draft out on a word processor, double-space between sentences, triple-space between paragraphs, and leave generous margins on both sides and at the bottom. This extra space will come in handy when you revise, edit, and rewrite the draft.

WRAPPING IT UP

The *conclusion* is the third and final part of a well-arranged communication, and it's often the most neglected part. In too many instances, we decide it's time to stop, and we "conclude" when we finish discussing a main idea. That's not a conclusion. It's more like quick kicking on third down or leaving a party without thanking the host and hostess.

An effective conclusion leaves the reader with a sense that you're justified in ending your communication. And you're ready to stop when you can assure your readers that you've accomplished the purpose stated in your introduction. In most writing, an effective conclusion summarizes the main points discussed in the body or resolves an issue. If you have a simple, straightforward purpose, you might want to emphasize it by restating it in slightly different words. But, if you have a complicated purpose or a long, involved communication, you'll probably need to emphasize your main ideas and state your proposals or recommendations. In some instances, a single recommendation is sufficient.

Many writers consider the conclusion a kind of "psychological close" designed to let readers know they've reached the end of the communication. Obviously, you shouldn't conclude with such statements as "I've reached the end of my discussion" or "That's all I've got to say." But restatements of main ideas, observations, or emphasis on main thrusts of arguments can make effective endings. In no case should you apologize for real or perceived inadequacies, inject weak afterthoughts, or make last-minute appeals for reader agreement. You should conclude your communication with positive statements based on your preceding discussion.

One of the most meaningful tests is to read your introduction and then follow immediately with a reading of your conclusion. This procedure can help you determine whether your conclusion flows logically from your introduction and whether it fulfills your purpose. An effective conclusion can point to broader implications, emphasize a need for action, or state a challenge for further action, study, or investigation. But, above all, it should convince your readers that you've reached a logical destination.

So much for a quick review of intros, bodies, and conclusions. Now, let's get back to curing the first-draft syndrome.

STICK TO IT

As you write your first draft, stick pretty close to your outline. Don't deviate. Don't revise. Don't polish. Don't mull over and reconsider aspects of the outline—yet.

DOUBLE-TIME DUMP

Write, type, or dictate quickly. Put those inky burps on paper as fast as they come! Compose as though you were talking to the potental reader. Spill your brains, don't worry about punctuation—just get it down in some form. If your outline is comprehensive, you may only need to string the ideas together with brief transitions. If your outline is merely a series of key words in a logical pattern, you'll have to fill in the larger blanks. Don't feel you need to start with the introduction; some writers do that section last. In any case, *get it down fast!*

DONE

If you've stuck to your outline and quickly filled in the blanks, you've just done it! Your first draft is ready for edit.

Wasn't that easy?
(. . .and what's an *edit*?)

"He throws away his best work."

Drawing by Bernard Schoenbaum
© 1974 *Saturday Review*

Get thy kit together!

Editing your work or helping someone else edit is a multifaceted challenge. Over 20 years ago, Jim Conley wrote an article for a government journal that highlighted several reasons why we fail to edit our work and clear up confused communication. Those reasons, adapted from Jim's article, are as valid today as they were then.

☞ We don't *really* read what we write. We may see the words, but that isn't the same as reading. We consciously overlook anything extra or omitted or inaccurate. What we think we just wrote is too firmly in mind to see that it isn't on the page. To solve this "blindness" we must proofread carefully and critically. Better yet, let somebody else proofread, or let a few days pass before you proofread yourself.

☞ We don't think we have a problem. We consider ourselves too intelligent or too simple or too average to have problems. Wrong! We are all susceptible. For example, writers have written such gems as these:

The car hit the deer in spite of its flashing lights and blaring horn.

The purpose of Mr. Moore's speech was to convince and inspire the college editors he was talking to that they should attempt to maximize satisfaction to themselves and to others while in the pursuit of excellence.

The cuisine is excellently prepared by qualified chefs ranging from tasty Maine lobster to corn-fed beef from Colorado.

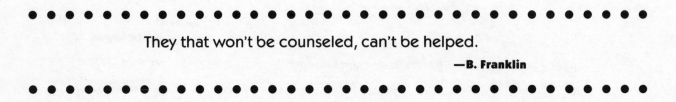

They that won't be counseled, can't be helped.

—B. Franklin

It makes no difference what degrees we've earned, what positions we hold, or how much experience we have; the basic problems of writing are problems for us all.

☞ We don't want to insult our readers. Some of us actually believe that readers who have above-average intelligence will be offended if our writing is too simple. Even if this were true, it doesn't show proper consideration for less fortunate readers. However, no one has ever been offended by writing that is easy to understand.

☞ We don't think clearly about what to write. Not long ago a teacher sat at his desk, apparently occupied, as he stared at the wall for about half an hour. A colleague came in and asked what was going on. The teacher replied, "I have to write a letter to all instructors for the boss' signature. It's about a new lesson procedure, and I don't know how to write it."

Drawing by N. A. Valencia (by permission)

● ●

Speaking or writing without thinking is like shooting without aiming.

—Arnold Glasow

● ●

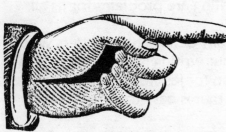

His colleague then asked, "What do you want to say?" The instructor told him. "Well, why don't you write what you just said?" It never occurred to the instructor that it could be so easy.

☞ We all tend to speak more fluently than we write. It is much easier, for example, to give a lecture (hard as that may be) than to write the same lecture as a paper for people to read. For some unknown reason, writing seems to tie up our thinking. The usual result is either wasted time or writing that is too vague, too general, too awkward, and too wordy.

Therefore, if the written words don't come easily, say aloud whatever it is you want the reader to know. Then write what you just said and polish as necessary.

☞ Finally, we are often too lazy or too busy to revise what we have written. We either don't proofread at all or else look back over our letters, reports, memos, or whatever and say, "My reader will know what I mean." Oh, really?

There is no more excuse for laziness in writing than in anything else. And there simply is no such thing as being too busy to proofread and rewrite, i.e.,

In addition to the fine work done by the Irish regiments he assured them that many a warm Irish heart beat under a Scottish kilt.

(From a London daily paper)

Maternity wear for the modern miss.

(Sign in a London store)

Split and warmed and served with our cheese, you will be the envy of your guests.

(From a catalog of a store in Sugar Hill, N.Y.)

• •

If it can be misunderstood . . . it will be.

—Murphy's Mother

• •

We have been "culturally conditioned" to write more words than we should. Think back to your high school, college, and/or graduate school days when you were given a writing assignment. Didn't the assignment always include *length* in pages or number of words? Did you *ever* get an assignment from a teacher or prof who simply said, "Adequately cover your topic in as few pages as possible; I'm interested only in clarity, brevity, and logical support." Can you imagine how much more effective we would be as writers today if all those teachers and professors who gave us assignments based on length would have had their mouths washed out with soap. (Show this paragraph to your child's English teacher!)

The real problem, then, is one of self-evaluation—understanding why we tend to act like we do. Numerous guides and checklists tell us how to get a grip on our bad habits, such as the above list of reasons for problems. The basic suggestion of all these guides is *think clearly about what you want to say.* Then write simply, write directly, and proofread carefully.

If we develop the habit of critical self-evaluation, all the problems cited here can be eliminated. Otherwise, they will continue to occur as often and as severely as they have in the past.

Once you've taken positive hold of your attitude and are convinced of the high utility in editing your work, you can begin.

RX FOR YOUR BABY

When you start to edit, you must shift from the role of writer to the role of critic. In a word, you stop feeding the child and begin examining it through the eyes of a would-be doctor. Your treatment depends on the condition of the patient. If the patient has only minor problems, the treatment may be a small shot in the arm. But you may face a problem requiring surgery. At any rate, don't begin the treatment until you evaluate the patient.

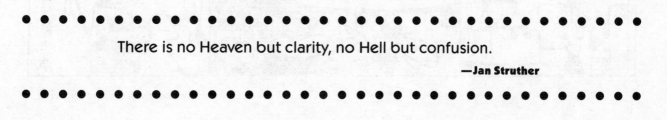

There is no Heaven but clarity, no Hell but confusion.

—**Jan Struther**

For effective evaluation, detach yourself emotionally from your material and look at it through "cold eyes." Changing to the "cold-eyes" approach involves two key actions—one physical and one mental. First, put the draft on a shelf, in a desk drawer, or under a paperweight, and let it "simmer" for awhile, preferably for several hours. Second, take some time to recall everything you've heard or read about writing. Your success in both actions will make it easier to evaluate your draft.

When you return to the draft, commit yourself to reading it a minimum of *three times.* These readings will not only strengthen the "cold-eye" but will also permit you to concentrate on different aspects of your writing.

FIRST: READ IT FOR TECHNICAL ACCURACY AND COVERAGE

Your primary concern in this reading is whether you have adequately covered your subject and whether you accomplished your purpose.

- *Have you included all information necessary for reader understanding? Have you correctly interpreted details and figures, if any? Do you need more supporting information? Have you made your point, and will your readers see it as you do? Are there factual gaps?*

This is the time to add information, move material to other paragraphs, or exchange positions of paragraphs. You can apply the same general questions and principles to one-paragraph letters and messages.

- *Don't hesitate to rewrite and revise when you feel it's necessary.*

Another concern is whether you've included irrelevant or too many details, or whether you've overwritten your subject. In either event, you may waste your readers' time, confuse them, or embarrass them with needless information.

- *Question and weigh all of your material and then decide whether you can delete, modify, or consolidate it.*

Your purpose is to include all information but not more than necessary for reader understanding and needs.

CROCK / *by Rechin & Parker*

Reprinted with special permission of NAS, Inc.

SECOND: READ IT FOR ARRANGEMENT AND FLOW OF IDEAS

For this reading, start with the "subject line," or title if the format you're using has such a thing. Decide whether it accurately reflects the substance of your communication. If it doesn't, now's the time to improve it. Remember, it should be specific, but broad enough to give readers a good idea of what they are about to read. It shouldn't be so long that they get lost in words, and it shouldn't be so short that it's meaningless. It's usually written as a complete sentence, especially a question. Test and experiment until it accurately reflects the content of your communication.

If your format does not carry a title or subject line, skip that step and test your introduction against the conclusion. Even if you're writing a short letter or message, you should give your readers the courtesy of an introduction and a "soft landing" at the end. Both the introduction and conclusion may consist of one sentence each. But the conclusion should echo the introduction and accurately reflect your purpose. Longer communications may or may not require more involved introductions and conclusions, but the same principles apply.

- *Does the introduction either suggest or state your precise purpose for writing? Does the conclusion show your readers you've accomplished your purpose? Do you "let your readers down" gradually? Or do you stop with a jerk?*

Revise as necessary.

When you're satisfied that your introduction and conclusion play their proper roles, you're ready to apply another test. Read the introduction again, and then read the topic sentences of all paragraphs between the introduction and the conclusion. This will give you a quick look at your main ideas as you move from the beginning to the end of your communication. It will also indicate the flow of ideas.

- *Are all topic sentences your main ideas about your subject? Are they major divisions of thought in support of your purpose? Do they move logically from point to point?*

Revise as necessary.

Now concentrate on your supporting sentences in each paragraph, beginning with the introduction. These sentences should expand, clarify, illustrate, and explain points mentioned or suggested in each main idea. And they should lead the reader in a smooth, step-by-step process from each main idea through your discussion to the next main idea. The last sentence in each paragraph should summarize points made in the paragraph, serve as a transition to the next main idea, or perform both functions.

● ●

If, at the close of business each evening, I myself can understand what I've written, I feel the day hasn't been totally wasted.

—**S.J. Perelman**

● ●

● *If you have any sentences that don't support main ideas, either delete them or revise them so they clearly play their proper roles. Do your ideas flow smoothly? Do all transitional words, phrases, and clauses improve the flow and show proper relationships? Do most paragraphs contain four to seven sentences?*

Revise as necessary.

THIRD: READ IT FOR READABILITY AND MECHANICS

Now you're ready to test the potential impact of your communication on your readers. Read the draft aloud and listen to the sound of words, phrases, and sentences. Some people even read what they've written backwards. (If it makes more sense that way, you should be writing campaign speeches or owner's manuals for electronic imports!) Seriously, it's a simple way to spot typographical errors.

In checking your writing for readability, always test it for simplicity and directness. The quicker your audience can read and understand it, the better. The most common barriers to simplicity and directness are these:

✍ Awkward, complicated arrangement of words and phrases

✍ Too many words and phrases

✍ Long, unfamiliar words rather than short, familiar words

✍ Passive, rather than active, expressions

✍ Monotonous sentences

✍ Misplaced modifying words, phrases, and clauses

These are common barriers, but there are others. In some cases, the problem may be a matter of grammar, mechanics, and natural versus unnatural expression. A review of the mechanics chapter will help you in all of these areas. They are the gremlins that destroy readable writing.

Your challenge is to inspect all statements. *Is there a simpler way to make a point? Did you use acceptable grammar? Are all ideas clearly stated? Have you applied standard practices in sentence construction and mechanics?* These questions are vital considerations in developing readable writing. Revise as necessary.

The three-part reading above is one application of the "cold-eye" approach, but time may limit your use of it. Even so, you can become familiar with it and use it as your time permits.

Regardless of the limits you have, you should read every rough draft at least three times and make necessary improvements before you "go final." After you become familiar with the principles discussed in the preceding paragraphs, you might use checklists to review and edit your work. There are many available, but the shortest one you'll ever find is on page 79.

SHOW 'N TELL

State your purpose to a fellow worker, review your analysis of the audience, and then show him or her your product. Ask for a brutal screening. Encourage your partner to *try* to misunderstand your communication—to put your work through a mental obstacle course.

DOUBLE-SPACE SAVES TIME AND DIMES

The old practice of sending the boss a letter-perfect copy is dying out. Many supervisors prefer a double-spaced draft to permit a final edit before publication. Secretaries generally prefer to type a double-spaced draft because it's quicker, easier, and particularly useful when more than one person must "hack" on the correspondence. Erasures, "white out," and sticky tape are also money savers when you're working a draft through the system, *unless you're using word processing equipment*. In that case you do *not* want to obliterate a word or phrase—you simply want to draw a line through it and write the change above it or in the margin. Word processing operators must be able to see the original words as well as the proposed changes/corrections.

If good things really do come in small packages, here's a helpful little item you can start using today. ➤➤

THE RAPID-FIRE
SHIRT-POCKET
FOUR-STEP
CUE CARD

☐ *Blockbusting*

Break the paper into organizational chunks—main points followed by support material. Identify the info which form whole units of data and treat them as a whole for all future editing.

☐ *Speed Shifting*

Quickly cut and paste. Reorganize blocks of material to provide continuity of thought and ideas—get the paper into logical arrangement.

☐ *Chopping*

Here's the fun part! Systematically and ruthlessly chop all "dead" words, extraneous phrases, redundancies, etc. Read paragraphs with some phrases and sentences left out—if you didn't really miss them—dump 'em!

☐ *Polishing*

Here's the easy job—once the info is arranged, organized, and chopped to the bare essentials, work on polishing the sentence structure and paragraphs. Work especially hard on word choice, transitions, and subject-verb agreements. When that's done—you're done!

THE LAST WORD ON EDITING

A "nitpicker" is the polite title for what General Billy Mitchell used to call a "pissant"—those people who can't resist changing someone else's writing.

Redoing anything takes time and material—which is money. Solid, conscientious editing, on the other hand, is crucial to effective communicating, and the time and material spent on it is worthwhile. It's the *other* kind of editing I'm highlighting here.

We have all worked for (or heard about) those individuals who can't leave anything the way it is. They would have said the *same* thing differently—and do—all over your work. It's a very easy trap to fall into, and this probably explains why so many of us have worked for nitpickers or have become one ourselves. It seems to rub people the wrong way when they are asked to sign something they did not help create. Psychologists give us other reasons like "pride of authorship," "bosses have to maintain their assumed superiority over subordinates," and a list of other theories that may or may not be appropriate.

The primary function of good editing is to ensure ideas being communicated are stated logically in acceptable English (correct grammar, easily understood words, phrases, paragraphs, and punctuation), and that the communication gets the point across in the fewest words. Editing is one of the important basic steps in building an effective communication.

Good editing calls for a certain mental perspective. Most people think they can edit someone else's work, but when someone cuts on *their* work, the supposed editor is often called a nitpicker. The editor may well be a nitpicker, but you should resist the temptation to categorize the editing. Look, instead, at the *content* of the editing. For example, if it corrects a grammatical error, clarifies a question, helps establish a desired tone, or chops unnecessary words, phrases, sentences, or even entire paragraphs, it is *good* editing rather than change for the sake of change.

Win a Few,
Lose a Few

Although I'll talk more about editing in the feedback section (just around the corner), let me leave you with this thought when you edit the work of others:

> *If the correspondence logically and concisely communicates the idea intended and is written in the appropriate tone with acceptable English, leave it alone!*

If, on the other hand, you're writing for a nitpicker, grin and bear it . . . .

FRUSTRATION BUILDS CHARACTER!

"The birthday cake we bought him had a typo in his name."

Saturday Review, 1975

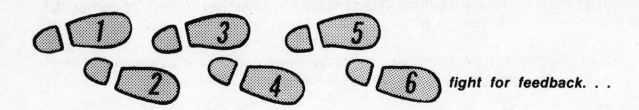

fight for feedback. . .

"must you corest every thing i say?"

Pine Point Syndicate

FEEDBACK
FEEDR
FEED
FEE

It's time to lift the blindfold,
pull out the earplugs,
open your mouth, and

FIGHT FOR FEEDBACK!

Feedback is a relatively new term for an old phenomenon. A synonym for feedback could be "reaction," and there certainly isn't anything new about folks reacting to each other. So why all the fuss about feedback?

The fuss concerns the philosophy that supports our reactions. The whole idea is that feedback should be given and received in such a way that we improve our communications. Unfortunately, for a great many of us, the basic idea of feedback is discomforting. As a rule, superior-subordinate relationships generate such a smoke screen of phony reactions that we find it a *real* challenge to close the communications loop.

WORKING WITH REVIEWERS AND SUPERVISORS

When you've done everything possible to improve your communication, you're likely to feel that it can't be improved any further. But, almost all of us are limited in our ability to criticize our own work. We become so personally involved in our purpose and subject that we tend to forget our audience. Don't permit pride of authorship and fear of criticism to close your mind to suggestions from other people. Your objective is to produce the most accurate and understandable communication possible.

• •

The mutual confidence on which all else depends can be maintained
only by an open mind and a brave reliance upon free discussion.
—Learned Hand

• •

The role of reviewers. Before giving the final draft or oral presentation to your supervisor, ask a fellow worker to read it, or listen to it, and suggest ways to improve it. If possible, give the draft or presentation to someone who understands writing or speaking problems and can identify problems of content, organization, and clarity. Explain the purpose of your effort and describe your audience. This information should give your reviewer the framework for offering suggestions.

If your reviewer suggests that your meaning isn't clear and explains why, you need to take another look at your material. Your supervisor and your audience may react the same way. After all, you respect the opinion and experience of your reviewer, or you wouldn't have asked for help. The reviewer's suggestions will be even more valuable if they pinpoint specific problems: wordiness, awkward sentences, unacceptable grammar, confusing visual aids, distracting mannerisms, and so on.

Remember: Your "cold-eyes" approach doesn't stop when you complete the final draft. It extends to your reviewer. The only way to ensure objective feedback is to accept whatever criticism comes your way. The reviewer is not only doing you a personal favor but is also representing your other readers or listeners. Ask for clarification, if necessary, but don't argue or defend yourself. Accept the reviewer's suggestions, and decide how you can best use them to improve your communication.

WHEN YOU'RE THE REVIEWER, SUPERVISOR, OR BOTH

An effective review is consistent, objective, and sensitive to the stated purpose. The ultimate test of the communication is the audience. Thus, when you review the communications of other people, try to distinguish between necessary changes, desirable changes, and unnecessary changes. Even in this role, you're committed to the "cold-eye" approach. Don't try to impose your style or personal preferences on the writing or presentations of others. (Remember what you just read about nitpickers?)

Responsibility as a supervisor requires tact and patience, especially in approving and disapproving the communications of subordinates. You know from your own experience that effective communicating is hard work. And any kind of writing or speaking requires concentrated effort. Thus, most people don't deliberately write poorly or fail to give a good speech or presentation because they're lazy. *As a supervisor, you are obligated to help your people improve their work.* This obligation may mean helping them to revise or rewrite their communication, especially if they are inexperienced. Whatever your role, tact and patience are key elements, and tact and patience come more easily to people once they really understand feedback in its broadest context.

The following ideas, adapted from an article by Richard S. Mayer in *Human Resource Management,* will provide additional insight into the necessity for feedback and our reluctance to fight for it.

☞ We are taught to be "polite," have the "right personality," manipulate ourselves and others, and play roles. Lots of energy thus goes into "managing communications," not saying what we really mean or feel. This creates incongruence in our communications; i.e., we send out mixed messages. People understand only part of what we say.

☞ We generally fear and avoid conflict. As a result, vast amounts of energy are wasted in circuitous communication. People fear conflict, fear that it will destroy working relationships. The granddaddy fear is that our opportunity for promotion will be derailed. If we challenge the conventional wisdom or ask for more specific instructions or suggest alternatives and our contemporaries *don't do any of that type of communicating,* then we hold back. We don't want to make waves; we throttle our imagination, our initiative, our true feelings. We may hide our confusion, our lack of understanding as to what the boss, or our workers, *really* want.

☞ We tend to draw conclusions, make assumptions, evaluate and judge rather than observe behavior and report what we see, hear, and feel.

☞ We usually aren't well in touch with ourselves. Our own stereotypes—daydreaming, fantasizing, self-image perpetuation, body feelings—contribute to the accuracy with which we can understand and communicate with others.

☞ We lack skills. We generally lack collaborative (cooperative) skills, but we do have well-developed competitive skills that get in the way of communication. Schools have tended to concentrate on one-way communication (making formal speeches), which is of little use in understanding face-to-face communication. A good supervisor, executive, or senior official *must become a master at consensus building.* The arts of suasion, logic, compromise, and real two-way understanding are essential to effective management and dynamic leadership.

Fortunately, we can greatly improve our ability to communicate through the use of feedback if we adopt new attitudes and learn new skills. For example:

☞ Learn to listen actively. Most of us have learned competitive listening skills; we listen selectively in order to influence or win an argument. We need to learn to listen for understanding. Listening for understanding means listening, without

evaluating, both to words and for feelings. It involves taking the risk of not mentally rehearsing what you are going to say, having the confidence you will know how to reply. Specific skills you can practice include feeding back to check out your understanding. Paraphrase what was said to you until the sender agrees you understand; i.e., "All right, Pete, if I understood what you said, you are suggesting that the conversion kits be. . ." (and so forth). Pete won't mind you paraphrasing his ideas and will appreciate the chance to check out *his* communication. Some people find it useful to listen with a note pad handy. When they think of something they want to say when the sender is finished, they make a brief note of it and return their full attention to the sender. Interrupt if necessary (and possible). Check out your perceptions to decode nonverbal messages.

☞ Become a more effective communicator. Look carefully at the person or people you are communicating with. If you sense through nonverbal communication that you're not getting across, paraphrase yourself or ask others to paraphrase. Describe your own feelings to help others decode your nonverbal signals. Shorten your messages and practice expressing yourself—especially your wants—more directly.

☞ Increase your awareness of yourself. This is the most useful, significant, and far-reaching action you can take. Also, depending on how deeply we are willing and able to explore, achieving self-awareness is by far the most difficult. You have to make yourself *available* for feedback—are you approachable?

By now, you're aware that feedback is a way to help yourself or another person change some specific behavior. Feedback is communication that helps individuals keep their behavior "on target." It helps one to achieve goals. Here are some criteria for giving or receiving useful feedback.

☞ Feedback should describe rather than judge. When we describe our reaction to another person's work, that person is free to use the feedback or not to use it, as he or she sees fit. Avoiding judgmental language reduces the other person's need to respond defensively.

☞ Feedback is both *positive* and *negative.* A balanced description of a person's work takes both the strong and weak points of the performance into account. Both types of feedback give useful information to the person who wants to change.

● ●

I have yet to find the man, however exalted his station, who did not do better work and put forth greater effort under a spirit of approval than under a spirit of criticism.

—**Charles Schwab**

● ●

☞ Feedback should be *specific* rather than general. General statements about another person's work do not indicate the performance elements that he or she may need to change and the elements that may serve as models.

☞ Feedback should take into account the needs of *both* the receiver and the giver of the feedback. What you say to a person about his or her performance reflects not only upon *his* or *her* work but also on *your* thinking or feeling about it at the moment.

☞ Feedback should be directed at *behavior that the receiver can control.* Only frustration results when a person is reminded of a shortcoming that he or she cannot control.

☞ Feedback should be analyzed to ensure clear communication. What the giver *intends* to say is not always synonymous with its *impact* on the other person. Ask about the meaning of doubtful feedback to clear up any discrepancy.

☞ Feedback should be *solicited* rather than imposed. Feedback is *most* useful when the receiver carefully formulates the kind of questions that will provide desired answers.

☞ Feedback should be directed at a person's *work* or *behavior,* not at the person.

The fight for feedback is tough work, but it can be instructive and particularly rewarding for those who wish to increase their capability as communicators.

"Now read that back to me."

© Vahan Shirvanian

"Nonsense!"

Drawing by Stevenson; © 1983
The New Yorker Magazine, Inc.

CHAPTER 3

The Tongue

GETTING IT OUT OF YOUR MOUTH

FUNCTIONS AND FORMATS FOR SPEAKING

This chapter describes a variety of functions and formats for spoken communication. Although functions and formats differ somewhat among various organizations, you will find the content useful in any situation.

TO SPEAK OR NOT TO SPEAK—THAT IS THE QUESTION

If you haven't done it already, the chances are good that you will eventually stand before an audience and talk. The prospect of making speeches or giving presentations usually causes knocking knees and sweating palms for all but the most experienced speakers. If you are an inexperienced speaker, the fundamentals of speaking contained in this section should help you solve these problems. If you are an accomplished speaker, use this as a review.

One goal should be to improve your self-concept as a speaker. To do this, you might begin now to think positively. Like writing and listening, speaking is a skill; once you grasp the basics, the rest is practice, polish, and style. You may be embarrassed by your initial mistakes, but you'll survive. Few of us will become great speakers, but all of us can become more effective if we take the time to practice the basics. Learn all you can from your contemporaries; some of them are accomplished speakers—you may be one yourself. If you are, share your views, tips, and personal hangups about speaking. Everybody improves to the extent that he or she "levels" with other people.

Before you consider those fundamentals unique to speaking, here's the whole enchilada one more time:

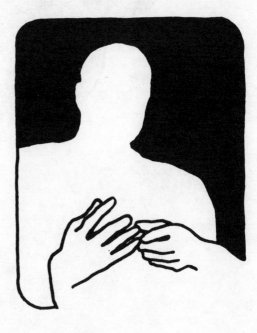

➻ 1. **Analyze purpose and audience**
➻ 2. **Conduct the research**
➻ 3. **Support your ideas**
➻ 4. **Get organized**
➻ 5. **Draft and edit with English that's alive**
➻ 6. **Fight for feedback**

Got it? Remember, those fundamentals are just as necessary for good speaking as they are for good writing. OK, here are the remaining fundamentals that are unique to verbal and nonverbal communication.

• •

The only rule that doesn't have its exception is this one.

—Herb Schwartz

• •

"I see that our next speaker needs no introduction."

Saturday Review, 1975

NONVERBAL COMMUNICATION

SWEATY PALMS SYNDROME

You must always be prepared to overcome stage fright. You can begin the first time you practice your speech. Know your first couple of paragraphs "cold." Usually, this includes the introduction and the transition into the first main point. This makes it much easier to get through the first and most difficult minute. Practice and plan to begin in a strong, self-assured voice. Be confident. Take a deep breath and survey your audience. Come on strong. Don't lose your audience in the introduction; otherwise, they may never hear your main points. Use natural gestures to relieve tension. Establish good eye contact with the audience and look for feedback (nods, puzzled looks). This search for feedback will take your mind off yourself and help you focus on the audience where your attention should be. Everybody experiences some degree of stage fright. Some people get a little nervous, and others become physically ill. In any event, don't apologize. Chances are the audience won't notice your nervousness if you don't mention it; if you call attention to your nervousness, your audience will become sensitive to it. Someone once said that every good speaker is nervous. The key is to make that excess energy work for you.

LOOKIN' GOOD

Another point in coming on strong is your appearance. Do you need a haircut? Are you distractingly overweight? Are your shoes shined? Is your suit clean and pressed? Have you dressed in good taste for the occasion? Your posture also creates a general impression of you as a speaker. Stand erect and alert, but don't be artificial. Don't lean on the lectern, rock back and forth or side to side, or slouch on one leg and then the other. Proper appearance builds confidence and reduces stage fright.

THE EYES HAVE IT

You should immediately establish eye contact with your audience. Let the members of the audience know you are looking at them and talking to them; don't stare, but at least look at them occasionally. This is the best vehicle for obtaining audience feedback and holding attention. A speaker buried in notes loses listeners. You can't wake 'em up if you don't know they're asleep.

PLAY YOUR FACE

Use facial expressions, but don't overdo them. Use them as if you are engaged in a casual conversation. You should not smile or frown continuously but as necessary to reinforce your speech and your points of emphasis.

GES-TIC-U-LATE

Gestures are another form of nonverbal communication. There is nothing magical about using your hands and arms. If you use them, make the movements natural. Make them add meaning to your speech. Practice meaningful gestures in front of your mirror. (If someone catches you in this act, plead the Fifth Amendment.)

THOSE FABULOUS FLIPS

Use visual aids to promote understanding of what you have to say. "A picture is worth a thousand words" is an old cliché that may be an understatement. Researchers tell us that a week after we hear a presentation *without* visuals, we have only retained about 5 percent of that data. When visuals are added, however, our retention is about 65 percent. Even allowing for the natural exceptions to any research, most of us would admit that "show 'n tell" has greater impact than "tell" alone. Examples of visual aids include objects, models, photos, maps, charts, and drawings, but use objects and models with caution. They are usually too small to be seen by the entire audience, and if you pass them around, they distract. Photos or drawings are usually better. The most universally used visual is the handy flip chart splattered with good old standard English. (And, of course, you are a *big* visual aid!)

• •

Who can refute a sneer?

—William Paley

• •

Photos, maps, charts, and drawings can be used on flip charts, overhead viewgraphs, 35mm projection equipment, and computer monitors. Make sure your visual aids project the image you want. If the photos are too large or too small, get a photo lab to fix them. If the drawings, sketches, or maps are not correct, contact the audiovisual section, if your organization has one, for an illustration to help you. These people are professionals who know how to prepare effective visual aids. Do this early to allow time for a quality product. Never say, "I know this is a poor visual aid, but . . . ." You'll turn the audience off, and you'll probably perform better if you omit the visual aid.

POOR PERSON'S GUIDE to CLASSICAL ART
WHAT? NO ART DEPARTMENT?! WELL, DON'T PANIC...

Gather together some wide *and* narrow felt tip markers in various colors (red, blue, green, and definitely black), an 18-inch wooden ruler or other suitable straight edge, and finally, something to flip: chart paper, butcher paper, poster board, commercial flip chart—you get the idea.

1 Take some scratch paper and jot down the basic facts and supporting data. Organize it for impact as you think about how you intend to present the briefing, speech, or presentation. Remember not to overload any flip chart page with too much data—5 to 8 lines on a flip chart is about maximum because your letters will have to be at least 1½ inches high for readability. After you've penciled up your scratch paper with the drafts of each flip and have the material organized the way you want it, it's time to reach for the markers.

2 Lay the straight edge down horizontally on the flip chart. Place the edge where you want the bottom of your top line to be. Pick up one of your wide felt tips and get ready to print.

3 Do all of your printing in *CAPITAL LETTERS* and bring the felt tip all the way down to meet the straight edge. You'll find that using the straight edge adds considerably to the appearance of your charts; capital letters enhance readability and neatness.

• •

Facial expression is human experience rendered immediately visible.

—Edmund Carpenter

• •

Quite often the time (or facility) is not available to have your visual aids professionally made. Don't despair. You can make your own, and there are many ways to do it. One of the quickest and cheapest is to use wide felt-tip markers, a ruler (for a straightedge), and a pack of flip-chart paper. This method is adequate for most small groups or desktop situations (see previous page for details). If you are facing a larger group, consider using viewgraphs, grease pencils, and acetate slides.

Desktop computers have ushered in a new generation of visual aid possibilities. You can use inexpensive production programs to create simple to complex visuals and either project the visuals to a large screen, print the visual in hard copy, or (with small audiences) use the actual monitor as your "flip chart" using the keyboard to call up the next visual aid. Here is a handy summary on the *use* of visual aids:

☞ Don't stand between your visual aid and the audience; make sure everyone can see.

☞ Don't talk to the visual aids; talk to the audience. Use a pointer, when necessary, to point out key items, and always point with the arm closest to the visual.

☞ Don't put up a visual aid until it is pertinent in your speech. After you use it, remove it or cover it up. This doesn't mean you shouldn't use a visual aid as an outline. In this case, you would leave it up for a longer period; but, again, when it's no longer useful, remove it.

☞ Make sure the visual aid is clear, simple, and readable. Busy visual aids are distracting, and if they cannot be read from the rear of the room they have no value. Check your visual aids for readability in the rear of the room before the presentation.

☞ Know your visual aid and immediately orient your audience to it. Have it labeled, if possible (i.e., "Top view of the engine intake," "Market analysis," "Horizontal output schematic").

☞ If you use an overhead or 35mm projector, ask another person to operate the equipment for you. This person should be familiar with your speech or with an outline that indicates when to project the visual aids.

☞ Visual aids provide a form of emphasis, but don't overdo them; when you emphasize everything, nothing receives emphasis. A good visual aid is a vehicle that makes a speech more understandable.

☞ Check *spellings* and *punctuation*!

☞ Don't read all the words on a chart, or you'll bore your audience.

☞ Unless you're a fairly skilled artist, keep the artwork simple and limit it to two or three colors (if you use color).

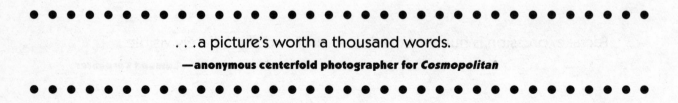

. . .a picture's worth a thousand words.
—**anonymous centerfold photographer for *Cosmopolitan***

VERBAL COMMUNICATION

How effectively do you use your voice to drive home your ideas or information? You have control over rate, volume, pitch, and pause. Use your voice to create interest in your presentation. Your voice can help you in the following ways.

RATE

There is no correct rate of speed for every speech. However, you might consider this fact: people can listen four to five times faster than the normal rate of 120 words per minute. If you speak too fast, your speech will be unintelligible, and if you speak too slowly, your meaning will suffer. If you do not vary your speed, you may lose the audience's attention. A faster rate notes excitement or sudden action, and a slower rate notes calm or fatigue. Use the rate of speech that adds emphasis to your presentation.

"Speak slowly. You know I don't understand gobbledygook."

Drawing by Bernard Schoenbaum
© *1974* Saturday Review

VOLUME

Volume is another verbal technique that can give emphasis to your speech. If possible, survey the room where you will make your presentation. Take time to talk in the room. Ask someone if you can be heard in the back of the room. Know how loudly you must talk. With the room filled, you will need to talk louder because the crowd will absorb the sound. If the audience must strain to hear you, they will quickly tune you out. Use a change in volume to emphasize a point. This can either be louder or softer. A softer level or lower volume is often the more effective way to achieve emphasis, assuming your listeners can easily hear you at a lower volume.

COMPUTER ERROR MERCHANDISE. Odd pages of manual, *Fly Your Own Helicopter*, and even pages of *Be Your Own Voice Teacher*, mistakenly printed, interspersed, and bound as one book. 11,000 copies offered at half-price.

PITCH

To use pitch effectively, you need to practice the talents of a singer. Pitch is really the use of notes (higher or lower) in voice range. Speak in a voice range that is comfortable for you and then move up or down the scale for emphasis. You can use pitch changes in vowels, words, or entire sentences. You can use a downward (high to low) inflection in a sentence for an air of certainty and an upward (low to high) inflection for an air of uncertainty. Variety in speech pitch helps to avoid monotone and rivets the listener's attention.

PAUSE

The pause gives you time to catch your breath and the audience time to collect your ideas. Never be in a hurry to give a speech; pause for your audience to digest your comments. The important question is this: Where do you allow time for your audience to reflect on your words? Pauses in speeches serve the same function as punctuation in writing. Short pauses usually divide points within a sentence, and longer pauses note the ends of sentences. You can also use longer pauses for breaks from one main point to another or from the body to the conclusion of your speech. However, don't get pause happy and make the speech sound choppy. For an excellent example of good technique, listen to radio and TV commentator Paul Harvey, the "Prince of Pause." Although a pause may seem long to you, it's usually much shorter than you think . . . and your audience will appreciate it.

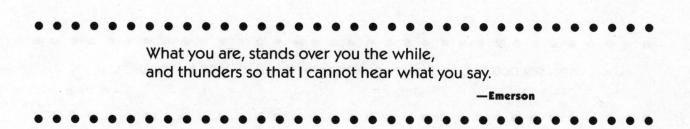

What you are, stands over you the while,
and thunders so that I cannot hear what you say.

—Emerson

ARTICULATION/PRONUNCIATION

You should consider two other points in your speaking: articulation and pronunciation; both indicate your oral command of the English language. Articulation is the art of speaking intelligibly and making the proper sounds with the lips, jaw, teeth, and tongue. Listen to yourself, and make your words distinct and understandable.

Of course, you can properly articulate a word and still mispronounce it. Unfortunately (and unfairly), many people consider word pronunciation or *mis*pronunciation a direct reflection on your intelligence. If you are not sure of your pronunciation, consult a current dictionary.

"HEY, WASSAMATTA?! DONCHA UNNASTAN DA KING'S ENGLISH?"

LENGTH

Length of presentation is crucial. Consequently, the basic foundation under all the points on how to organize and present your verbal communications is an admonition—be brief and concise. There are few people who will tolerate a speaker who wastes the audience's time. Have your stuff together before you speak. Know what you want to say and say it.

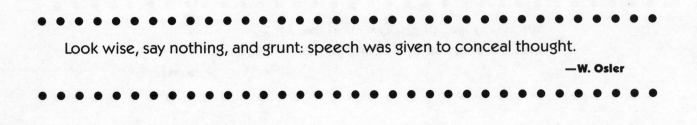

Look wise, say nothing, and grunt: speech was given to conceal thought.

—W. Osler

"What's all the hoopla about?"

© 1974, 1989 Jack Ziegler and *Saturday Review*

PRACTICE ALOUD

We are probably the worst judges of the quality of our own speeches. Practice the speech or presentation in front of a critical listener, if possible. Do a dry run at the office or in the room where you will make your presentation. Do your visual aid machines operate? Is there a smooth flow? Make the speech appear natural. Know your delivery style and techniques before you practice too much. A tape recorder and full-length mirror may be helpful.

Well, that's it. If you've used the basic checklist for developing your material and if you follow the fundamentals of verbal and nonverbal communication outlined above, you'll be able to give a credible pitch.

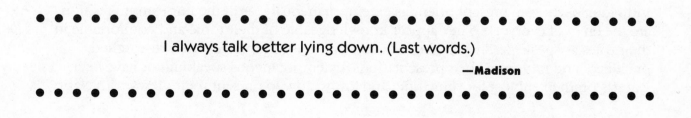

I always talk better lying down. (Last words.)

—Madison

EXTEMPORANEOUS OR IMPROMPTU?

ex tem′ po ra′ ne ous

> Composed, performed or uttered on the spur of the moment; impromptu; hence, spoken without notes or reading or being memorized.
> –Webster's New International Dictionary

> Delivered in an apparently spontaneous manner, although detailed planning, outlining, and practice precede it; not delivered by rote memory. Differs from impromptu speaking in that considerable time exists for preparation.
> –Schwartz' New Intergalactic Dictionary

Although Noah Webster didn't distinguish between extemporaneous and impromptu speaking, he *should* have. (Who can blame him—he was a writer—not a speaker!) *Impromptu* speaking is what we do when asked to respond during a meeting or when we are asked to take the floor at a conference, etc. It's what we do when we have to speak publicly *without warning* or on a few moments' notice. To do it *well* requires a great amount of self-confidence, mastery of the subject, and the ability to think on your feet. A superb impromptu speaker has achieved the highest level in verbal communications.

Extemporaneous speaking, on the other hand, refers to those times when we are given *ample opportunity to prepare*. This doesn't mean that we write a detailed script and then memorize every word of it, but it *does* mean that a good extemporaneous speaker will carefully plan and practice the presentation. A thorough outline provides the necessary foundation. The specific words and phrasing used at the time of delivery, however, are basically spontaneous and sound very natural. Speech professor David E. Steiner sums it up:

> *The result of extemporaneous or impromptu speaking, at its best, is an illusion of spontaneity which clearly differentiates it from the manuscript or memorized speech. It also allows for the use of feedback. I try to stress that the impromptu speech is not (or shouldn't be) a result of* no *preparation. Mastery of the six steps in T&Q should give you, even if you have only a few seconds, the ability to put your thoughts in some sort of coherent order—to make some judgments about the audience, to decide on main points and support. A few lines on a note pad or ten seconds of serious thought represent preparation, and that is the key to successful communication.*

Individuals who can present briefings extemporaneously, or in the impromptu fashion, are the envy of everyone. They appear knowledgeable of their topic and comfortable in their roles as speakers. They are both of these because they have either researched, practiced, and rehearsed their presentations (extemporaneous speaking) or have been experts on their subject for some time and know how to present their views with clarity on a moment's notice (impromptu speaking). They think carefully before they speak, outline their main ideas, say what has to be said, conclude, and shut up. They actually *enjoy* it. It's a challenge, and it allows them to be more direct, spontaneous, and sensitive to feedback than any other delivery technique.

Actually, when we're not listening, sleeping, or thinking, we're spending most of our time in extemporaneous or impromptu speaking. The big difference comes when we get up in front of a group, a senior decisionmaker, or a client and present our ideas. Assuming you have your stuff together (a *crucial* assumption), the more often you speak in front of or with a group, the more self-confident you will become. High confidence and thorough knowledge of your subject are important prerequisites for extemporaneous or impromptu speaking.

Speeches grow and mature. They need time to ripen, and they require constant cultivation. Some people find this incredible. "Good speakers," they argue, "can talk off the cuff." That notion, of course, is sheer fantasy.

—**J. Jeffery Auer**

It usually takes more than three weeks to prepare a good impromptu speech.

—**Mark Twain**

". . . on my seventh point, I'd like to begin by saying. . . ."

N. A. Valencia (by permission)

AN INTRODUCTION TO THE ORAL PRESENTATION

In the preceding sections, I reviewed basic speech fundamentals and impromptu or extemporaneous speaking. Now we zero in on the formal presentation.

There are as many different types of presentations as there are professions, but I highlight three: the presentation to inform, the presentation to persuade, and the manuscript presentation.

Before we cover these three types of presentations, I offer one point about formality and informality. *Formal* presentations tend to be the rule rather than the exception at higher organizational levels. Formats are prescribed, time limits are set, and the contents of the presentations are coordinated with all parties involved.

● ●

Speaker to audience: "I've practiced this speech all week and I feel pretty good about it. So, if you could just manage to look a little more like a bathroom mirror, we'll begin."

—**Robert Orben**

● ●

Written guidelines or "office tradition" will generally provide the technical information necessary for you to prepare your formal presentation. As a matter of fact, they may even include rules for colors to use in visual aids. They may also require written copies of your presentation, either in manuscript form or in extensive background notes.

If you use background notes, they should contain detailed information because you may give the presentation at various echelons before you make your final presentation. With extensive background notes, you can be sure you present information that was agreed upon at intermediate levels.

Informal presentations are given at all organizational levels. Such presentations may involve routine status reports at periodic gatherings. More typical at higher levels are "desktop" discussions, which also tend to be extemporaneous in nature. These usually come in response to phone calls from senior staff asking that you stop by and "fill in the boss."

In "desktop" situations, you may need to organize quickly, grab any available graphics, run up to the boss' office, and speak extemporaneously. You may find appropriate viewgraphs in your office files, or you may have a few moments to prepare a flip chart for your presentation. Many effective staff members and department heads anticipate requirements and prepare short informal visual aids ahead of time. The "fill-in" type prepared with acetate over poster board can be quite helpful. Computer-generated graphics are also very popular.

Your ability to make oral presentations informally and extemporaneously depends on your talent, effort, and, to some extent, the environment in which you operate. At lower levels, you may make many informal presentations. At higher levels, you may have limited opportunities to do so, although higher levels have definitely shifted toward informality during the past several years.

If you have an option, I suggest the informal style. It's more professional and less stilted and carries the greatest potential for an open exchange of information and personal views.

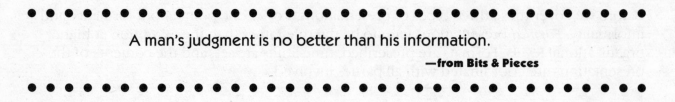

● ●

A man's judgment is no better than his information.

—**from Bits & Pieces**

● ●

THE INFORMATIVE PRESENTATION

The purpose of this presentation is to inform the listener (amazing!). This type of presentation deals only with facts; it has no place for recommendations. A good informative presentation should include a short introduction indicating the topic to be presented; the body, stating the facts clearly and objectively; and a short summary, depending upon the length of your presentation and the complexity of your subject matter.

When you make an informative presentation, you must, of course, be as brief and to the point as possible. At the same time, you should anticipate some of the questions that may arise and treat them in your remarks. Since you cannot anticipate all questions, try to have enough background information available to satisfy your interrogators. If you cannot answer a question, do *not* attempt to snow the questioner with some off-the-top-of-the-head answer. That kind of response may come back to haunt you. Admit you don't know the answer, and offer to provide it later.

Reprinted with special permission of *King Features Syndicate, Inc.*

• •

The silence often of pure innocence persuades when speaking fails.

—Shakespeare

• •

Drawing by N. A. Valencia (by permission)

THE ADVOCACY PRESENTATION

You can fill a bookshelf with masterful works on "How to Persuade," and college catalogs cough up numerous courses on debate, advocacy, persuasion, and salesmanship. Our entire society is, in fact, modeled on advocacy. The executive, congressional, and judicial branches are argumentative counterbalances to each other. The extent to which we can effectively move our organizations forward is a direct function of advocacy between, and within, our company or institution, competing organizations, various regulatory bodies or commissions, stockholders or special interest groups, and society at large.

At some level and in some fashion, you advocate something to someone almost every day. You probably don't recognize the skill and experience required to advocate successfully

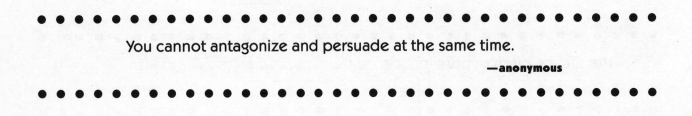

You cannot antagonize and persuade at the same time.

—**anonymous**

until you come up against a really tough customer. *The Tongue and Quill,* at least up to this point, has been designed to aid you in getting your story together—and presenting it with greater impact. I've also talked about how to interpret that other fellow's song and dance. What remains, then, is to illuminate some of the finer points of persuasion.

COMPLEXITY

Persuasion or advocacy is an incredibly sophisticated and complex process. It involves more variables than I care to catalog, and many of those variables are uncontrollable. Some examples of those variables include the time dimension, consensus building, and the ego states of the communicative participants. I mention the complexity of advocacy for no other reason than to warn you that the best of persuasive efforts may sometimes fail, and the worst may succeed for any number of factors outside the immediate control of the advocator. So be it. Now, let's go a buttonhole lower to those factors you *may* be able to control.

CREDIBILITY

The most important ingredient in advocacy is the aura surrounding the advocator. It's a fluid composite of personality, appearance, knowledge of subject, sensitivity, integrity, organization, preparation, approach, good will, and at least a dozen other things. Notice I said a *fluid* composite. You can gain or lose credibility at any moment, and you can probably tick off a handful of reasons on how that could happen.

Are you the kind of person people *enjoy* agreeing with, or are you the type they might enjoy *refusing*? Think about it. Introspection can be the most important aspect of persuasion.

SETTING

What's the best place to persuade or advocate? If you control the location of your presentation or discussion, arrange things to your advantage. A conference table is great if discussion is needed. If you expect strong opposition, a small auditorium inhibits spontaneous discussion and may be best in such circumstances.

How about the boss' office? In *Perspectives on Persuasion*, W. C. Fotheringham shows that it is more difficult for cabinet officers or political representatives to say "no" in the President's oval office or study than in a more neutral environment. Would this research finding apply to your presentation? It might. The boss' office could lend status to your efforts.

The setting also includes the carpetbagger concept—"He who leaves his home court is at a disadvantage." If you have the option, invite your audience to come to you, particularly if you expect a fight. You'll be more comfortable, and they'll be slightly off their psychological balance. Don't gamble on it making a big difference; it's just another consideration.

TIMING

If you want the members of your audience full of spark, advocate in midmorning. If you want them impatient and anxious, advocate just before lunch. If you want them agreeable, advocate immediately after lunch; if you want them asleep, try midafternoon; finally, if you like pressure politics try the "just before quitting time tactic." The adversary may collapse in agreement just to catch the car pool. Remember, these are merely *general* tendencies in behavior. Don't count on the predictability of human dynamics.

ORGANIZE FOR RESULTS

Here are the four common ways to organize material when you attempt to persuade:

Reason pattern is simply the use of examples to support or defend a point of view or idea. (This is also called the inductive pattern.)

General-to-specific pattern is the process of generalizing from one experience in order to advocate a specific action in another situation; for example, get agreement on some general point—e.g., "Driver's training produces a generally safer driver." Then you move to your specific point—e.g., "We need to send all our drivers through driver's training." This is an overly simplified example, but you get the point. The key is to be certain you show the logical relationship between the generalization and the specific; maybe those who are *forced* to take driver's training would show different results than those who *volunteer* for the course. (The general-to-specific pattern is a form of deductive reasoning.)

- -

There is a holy mistaken zeal in politics as well as in religion.
By persuading others, we convince ourselves.

—anonymous

- -

Problem-solution pattern is analogous to a verbal feasibility study. Each possible solution is evaluated as to how well it meets the criteria, and the speaker concludes by identifying the best solution. A frequent variation to this pattern consists of giving the decisionmaker *only* the solution you feel is best. (Thus, you don't waste time with previously discarded alternatives.)

Psychological pattern is when you lead the listener along a psychological path. You proceed through five steps: attention, need, satisfaction, visualization, and action. For example, in persuading an audience to support a statewide prenatal-care bill, you may call *attention* to the high rate of infant mortality among the target group. You will then emphasize the *need* for better prenatal care by showing the long-term social and monetary costs of inadequate care and why present methods of care are not effective. In the *satisfaction* step, you may point out that other states have controlled the problem of infant mortality through increased funding and improved public health programs. In the *visualization* step, you may outline a proposed bill for the state. And, in the *action* step, you can suggest steps for your audience to take in persuading the legislature and health department to enact the bill.

• •

The wise are instructed by reason; ordinary minds by experience; the stupid, by necessity; and brutes, by instinct.

—Cicero

Reminds me of a guy I once worked for.

—Schwartzo

• •

Choose the organization pattern you feel will be most persuasive and one you feel comfortable with. Which one would help convince *you*? You can combine part of the above patterns or develop new patterns.

FINAL TIPS ON VERBAL SWORDPLAY

➡ As a general rule, present both sides of the argument. Research indicates that 60 percent of the listeners will lean toward your argument when you present *both* sides, whereas only 5 percent of the listeners will give you the nod when you present only your side.

➡ Don't play cat and mouse with the listeners. Explain at the beginning where you hope to end up. Those advocators who hold on to the punch line till the very end are only trying the patience of the audience. Tell them where you're going, and let them reason along with you.

➡ It's generally best to move *from the familiar to the new* and *from the simple to the complex*.

➡ Build toward a logical and compelling climax. Points made near the end of a presentation generally have greater impact on an audience, so save your magnum shots for the finale.

➡ Use the conclusion to clearly restate your position and the pertinent support. Reinforce your ideas.

➡ Anticipate questions. Many a good advocacy goes down the tubes in the question-and-answer session. Why? Most often, the advocator cannot handle the questions because of a lack of knowledge. Know your subject! No more sage advice could ever be given a presentor in an advocacy situation. But what about questions that come *before* you are finished speaking? Most of us know this is the rule rather than the exception. If you can't respond to an interruptive question and smoothly recover, you're in trouble. The ability to move in and out of your presentation without "clanking up" is essential to effective advocacy. *Expecting* and *anticipating* interruptions is a helpful mental attitude.

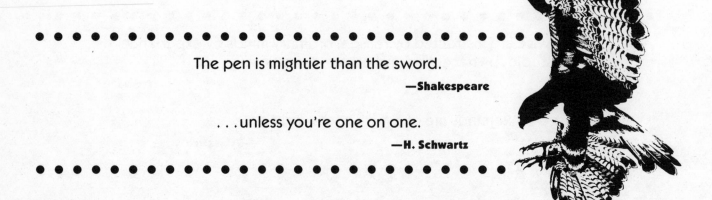

• •

The pen is mightier than the sword.

—Shakespeare

. . .unless you're one on one.

—H. Schwartz

• •

Practice is the best of all instructors.

—**Publius Syrus**

Better slip with foot than tongue.

—**Benjamin Franklin**

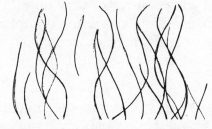

A universally endorsed recipe for improving your speaking ability is to run, don't walk, to the nearest Toastmasters club. Many cities have an active chapter. In a spirit of fun and helpfulness, usually during a monthly luncheon, fellow members will put you in the skillet—you'll stand up, give a short presentation, and then get critiqued. Along with the materials you'll read and the opportunity to hear and critique other members, your confidence and competence as a public speaker will undergo a change more positive than you ever thought possible. It sure beats stepping on your tongue!

New opinions are always suspected, and usually opposed, without any other reason but because they are not already common.

—**Locke**

THE SCRIPTED PRESENTATION

In his *Executive's Guide to Effective Speaking and Writing,* Frederick L. Dyer refers to the scripted presentation or manuscript briefing as "Speak-Reading." A script ensures you get it right every time. Scripted presentations are often used at high management levels when complex or controversial issues are involved. Repercussions and embarrassment caused by a speaker's inadvertent ad-libbing can be crippling to the cause.

A word of caution concerning the use of scripts: they make presentation a piece of cake, right? Wrong. In delivering a scripted presentation, many people demonstrate a tendency toward monotone and a general lack of spontaneity. They lack eye contact with the audience and stand behind the lectern with the script lying before them. Adequate preparation can eliminate these barriers to communication.

Preparation of a scripted presentation involves the same fundamentals as any other speech. The phraseology should reflect your normal speaking habits. You should avoid stilted wording and phrase technical terms in easily understood language. If a speech typewriter (extra large letters) is not available, you should prepare the script in double- or triple-spaced format and type it in all capital letters. Use a highlighter pen to accentuate certain words/phrases for vocal emphasis. The script should be assembled to facilitate easy reading. A three-ring binder may fill the bill for you, but you may find you distract your audience less by stacking numbered pages as you read them rather than flipping them in a binder. If you have visual aids, mark your script with red dots where slide or chart changes should occur.

In practicing for a scripted presentation, you should become so familiar with the words that you can naturally add the ingredients of volume, inflection, and eye contact to your presentation. After you read the script to yourself, stand up and read it aloud. You will find you can remember key phrases, which will be helpful when you must leave your script to point out details on a visual aid.

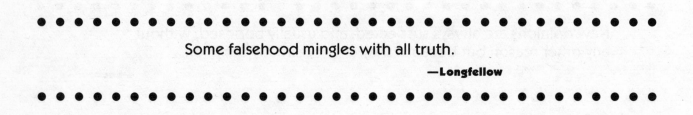

Some falsehood mingles with all truth.

—Longfellow

To summarize some of the key points in preparing and presenting a scripted presentation, let's assume you have scrambled through the six-step checklist and are now ready to prepare a working draft.

➟ Write as if you were speaking:
—Use contractions
—Keep sentences and paragraphs relatively short
—Make transitions more explicit
—Freely repeat key words
—Use personal pronouns, if appropriate
—If you get into abstract or complicated reasoning, follow with specific examples

➟ Rehearse, curse, and rehearse:
—Read and reread until you've practically memorized it
—Avoid combinations of words that are difficult to say
—Look at your audience when uttering emphatic words and during the closing words of a sentence
—Preplan gestures—strive for enthusiasm and naturalness
—Dry run your visuals

➟ Final draft preparation:
—Use a speech typewriter or the largest type available; all caps
—Double- or triple-space
—Number pages with bold figures
—Underscore words you wish to emphasize, and insert vertical marks where you plan a major pause

➟ Closing tips for the totally confident:
—Never explain why you choose to read
—Be flexible; if necessary (and appropriate), know where you can shorten the speech and where you might insert impromptu remarks to add spontaneity

If you can deliver a scripted presentation without error and still maintain a natural and direct contact with your audience, you have a masterful command of "Speak-Reading."

Drawing by Lorenz; © 1976
The New Yorker Magazine, Inc.

When he stands up to speak, battalions of words march out of his mouth and scour the countryside in search of an idea; and when they find one, they promptly trample it to death.

—**an anonymous cabinet member of President Warren G. Harding**

THE TELEPHONE

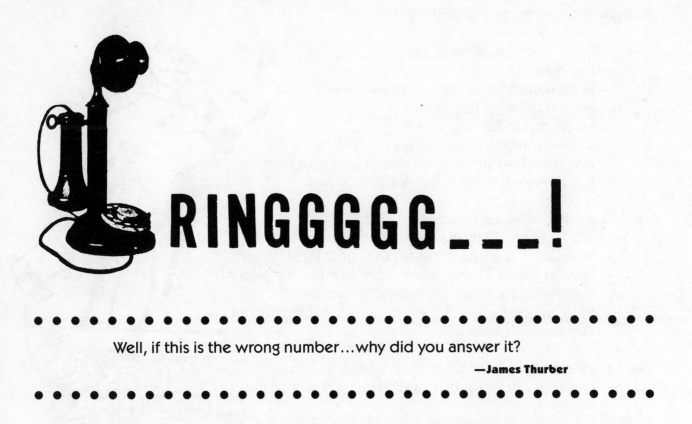

RINGGGGG___!

Well, if this is the wrong number...why did you answer it?

—James Thurber

Technologically, the telephone is in its adolescence. Patents have already been registered for advanced uses of the telephone with existing facilities—phonovision, voting by phone, access to computer assistance with the telephone as a digital keyboard, microrecordings of conversations for later retrieval, and wireless handheld instruments that can connect the holder to any phone system in the world. These are only a few of the advances that have already been developed—and some have been applied.

Who knows what's around the corner in new concepts? Still, the basic function of the telephone hasn't changed. We use it to communicate ideas, and many of us use it more than any other communications instrument.

Effective use of the phone requires an organized approach. Have you ever had a conversation with a caller only to hang up and think, "What did he say?" Or have you finished a call and realized that you forgot to get all the information?

How sweet and gracious, even in common speech, is that fine sense which men call courtesy!

—J. T. Fields

Most of us are bright enough to handle the obvious common courtesies of phone talk, such as "Hi, this is Franco Franchini. Is Miss Blivitzsk there?" But other courtesies, such as the following, are not so obvious:

☎ Asking whether the person has time to talk if you plan a lengthy conversation.

☎ Planning and organizing your thoughts before you place a call; perhaps listing the points you need to cover on a note pad.

☎ Taking a number and calling back if the call is intended for someone else rather than leaving the caller hanging while you search for a number.

☎ Allowing the person initiating the call to terminate the call.

☎ Returning telephone calls as promptly as possible.

☎ Making the call as brief as possible. Don't tie up expensive long-distance (or any lines for that matter) with long-winded bull sessions.

☎ Giving more attention to *preparing* to communicate. Without the benefit of nonverbal feedback, telephone conversation requires greater sensitivity.

☎ Recording your conversation in a memorandum and placing it in the appropriate file. Don't trust your memory on important subjects.

☎ Assigning someone to screen calls. Incoming calls are highly distracting and can be managed more effectively if there is someone assigned to screen all calls. Communications researchers estimate that as many as 70 percent of incoming calls request information that can be provided by someone other than the boss.

You can probably offer other tips for more effective use of telephones; these should stimulate your thinking about this important instrument.

"Hello, is that you, Edward? Listen, I'm sorry but I can't talk to you now. Wait a minute! Did you call me or am I calling you? Will you hold or should I? Better yet, why not leave your name and number and we'll get back to you later."

ACTIVE LISTENING

LEND ME YOUR EARS

Historically, listening has taken a back seat to other aspects of the communicative process. Only in recent years have we started to *listen* to this problem of listening . . . and how to understand that person at the other end.

In the next few pages, three quotations from Allan Katcher in *Experiences in Being* are used to illustrate how we err with our ears. After each quotation, I describe a situation that should bring the chickens home to roost.

> *A friend of mine, Elias Porter, has made me realize vividly why I don't often listen. He says that we often hear what other people are saying, but we do not fully tune in because we are so busy thinking about what is said. He believes that the most important hindrance to active listening is that we fail to acknowledge what the other person has tried to get across to us. For example, while another person is talking, we think about him. We try to evaluate the worth of his words, seek for deep motivations, and make judgments about the person and what he is saying, rather than understanding where he is.*

The true art of memory is the art of attention.

—Johnson

Does the following conversation sound familiar? "Filling out these forms in quadruplicate is dumb," the clerk said. And I thought to myself, Why can't he just do what he's told instead of always badmouthing procedures? Maybe he's just lazy. I said, "There must be a good reason; those other agencies would scream if they didn't get their copy." He mumbled something obscene and turned back to his typewriter.

A week later, I was sitting in the boss' office. Someone higher up had suggested we screen all requirements for duplicate, courtesy, and info copies. The boss turned to me, "I'll bet we could save a bundle in paper if we took a critical look at some of our administrative procedures. What do you think?" "No doubt about it," I replied. "In fact, just the other day one of my clerks was saying. . . ."

But was anyone *listening*? When we stack enough status on top of an idea, it's surprising how quickly we support the thought. How many communications get fogged up because we barely hear them through the filters of status or prejudgment? We think about the *clerk* rather than his *ideas*. (And perhaps it's easier to make an excuse than to take the time to question routine.)

> *Sometimes we try to* think for *the other person; that is, we try to find solutions for his problem or mentally try to direct his activities. . . . So often when we want to help others we shortchange them and minimize the seriousness of their problems by thinking for them, by having a solution in mind before they have a chance to describe all the feelings and ideas they might have. It is sad to say, but unless somebody asks for help, such thoughts only tend to turn them off, to make them feel worthless and uncared for.*

One of our occupational hazards is a penchant for problem solving. Grab the issue, take charge, and solve it! In moving from one crisis to the next, like so many public health doctors chasing after the furtive shadows of a thousand Typhoid Marys, we seldom take the time to *listen* for all the symptoms, much less the causes.

> *Another hindrance to active listening—an attitude which I am afraid I engage in—is* thinking ahead, *mentally jumping forward to get the story over with before the other person is halfway there. I say to myself that, because I am an intuitive and sensible individual, what I am doing is probably correct. My impatience does not help. I can't help noticing that my friend Porter is right—that when I do this, the other person seems bothered, frustrated, and that in some way I have really missed the message.*

> *On the other hand, I have to tell you how good it feels when people really listen to me, when I sense they have understood and appreciated the full, rich complexity of what I have tried to share with them. Porter calls this* thinking with *a person. . . .*

> *People think with me in lots of ways: often by looking at me while I am talking or by nodding, sometimes by mirroring in their expressions some of the thoughts I am expressing or aptly summarizing in a brief remark the essence of what I have said, without jumping* ahead *of me! That is a wonderful feeling. It is as if they are telling me that* they really understand how I feel; how things look to me, through me.

Does that sound familiar? It should. Allan Katcher described, in a very personal way, one of the real payoffs from feedback. Getting and giving meaningful feedback depends heavily on listening. But, as described above, active listening is difficult because of the three barriers Allan Katcher so aptly described: (1) we *think about the speaker* instead of what he's *saying;* (2) we *think for* the other person instead of allowing him to seek his *own* solution; (3) we *think ahead* of the speaker instead of thinking *with* him.

Here are seven additional "do's" for good listening:

➥ **Do. . .make and (sometimes) hold eye contact.** Let the talker know you care about what's being said. If the speaker prefers not to hold eye contact, act as though you're waiting patiently.

➥ **Do. . .tune out your own ideas.** You can't really consider the other person's ideas if you fill your head with your own ideas. This requires humility, and it tests your ability to listen actively.

➥ **Do. . .synthesize what's being said.** Remember, the speaker may have a great idea in mind but may not be expressing it properly. Listen to the concept—what the person is really trying to say—not just to the words.

➥ **Do. . .listen to understand,** not to refute or question. If you listen to refute or to question, you'll frequently find that you don't understand the idea at all. You really can't *refute* until you *know.* Question, refute, or doubt the material *after* you finish listening.

➥ **Do. . .take notes with care.** Taking notes can be flattering to the speaker if you take only a few good notes. But, if you take notes continuously, the speaker is likely to feel that too much material is being covered or that your extensive notes will be used as a trap. In either case, the speaker will be thrown off balance.

➥ **Do. . .keep your feelings positive.** If you distrust or doubt a speaker, it will show on your face. If you control your negative predisposition toward the subject (or the speaker) and strain to accept what you hear, you may actually change your mind!

➥ **Do. . .prove that you are a good listener** by absorbing new ideas and crediting the source as you pass them on. No one stands taller than those who display the good sense to recognize the virtues of new ideas and the honesty to credit their sources.

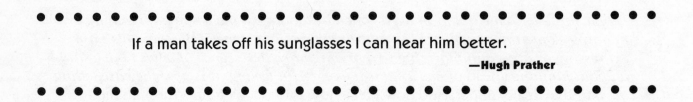

● ●

If a man takes off his sunglasses I can hear him better.

—Hugh Prather

● ●

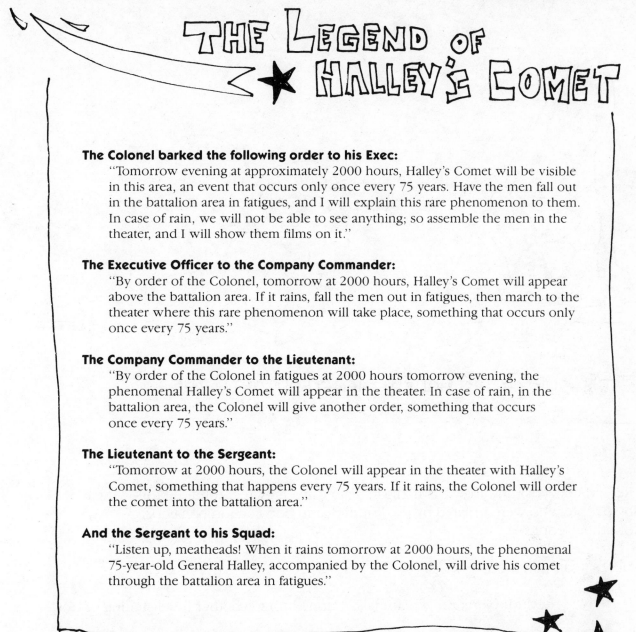

THE LEGEND OF HALLEY'S COMET

The Colonel barked the following order to his Exec:

"Tomorrow evening at approximately 2000 hours, Halley's Comet will be visible in this area, an event that occurs only once every 75 years. Have the men fall out in the battalion area in fatigues, and I will explain this rare phenomenon to them. In case of rain, we will not be able to see anything; so assemble the men in the theater, and I will show them films on it."

The Executive Officer to the Company Commander:

"By order of the Colonel, tomorrow at 2000 hours, Halley's Comet will appear above the battalion area. If it rains, fall the men out in fatigues, then march to the theater where this rare phenomenon will take place, something that occurs only once every 75 years."

The Company Commander to the Lieutenant:

"By order of the Colonel in fatigues at 2000 hours tomorrow evening, the phenomenal Halley's Comet will appear in the theater. In case of rain, in the battalion area, the Colonel will give another order, something that occurs once every 75 years."

The Lieutenant to the Sergeant:

"Tomorrow at 2000 hours, the Colonel will appear in the theater with Halley's Comet, something that happens every 75 years. If it rains, the Colonel will order the comet into the battalion area."

And the Sergeant to his Squad:

"Listen up, meatheads! When it rains tomorrow at 2000 hours, the phenomenal 75-year-old General Halley, accompanied by the Colonel, will drive his comet through the battalion area in fatigues."

We seldom hide our mental barriers to good listening from those who attempt to talk with us. Sometimes what we do may *appear* as a barrier when we don't really intend it to be. The whole spectrum of communications—body language, active listening, feedback—is loaded with opportunities to misread signs and symbols. That's what makes the communication process such a frustrating and fascinating affair.

● ●

Next to entertaining or impressive talk, a thorough-going silence manages to intrigue most people.

—Mrs. J. Borden Harriman

● ●

"I'M SICK OF HIS 'HOLIER-THAN-THOU' ATTITUDE..."

Researchers Posz and Dow of Michigan State University recorded the following remarks by people who were irritated by the listening and body-action behavior of other people.

Here's a sampling:

- "...never looks at me when I talk. I don't know whether he's listening or not."

- "...continually fidgets with a pencil, a paper, or something, looking at it or examining it as if studying *it* rather than listening to me."

- "...sits there picking hangnails, clipping or cleaning fingernails, or cleaning glasses, etc."

- "...keeps rummaging through papers on her desk, or through her desk drawers."

- "...keeps looking at his watch or the clock on the wall."

- "...doesn't sit still."

- "...walks away when I'm talking."

- "...has such a poker face and manner that I never know whether he's listening or whether he understands me."

- "...acts as if she's doing me a favor in listening to me."

- "...never smiles; I'm afraid to talk to him."

- "...always trying to get ahead of my story."

- "...asks questions as if she doubts everything I say."

- "...asked questions as if he didn't hear what I had said earlier."

- "Everything I say reminds her of an experience, a happening, a story."

- "When I'm talking, he finishes sentences or supplies words when mine don't come fast enough for him."

Who me?

Who *else*.

"What? I'm sorry. I wasn't listening."

Jack Ziegler

MEATY
MEETINGS

MEATY MEETINGS

A massive amount of time is misused every day by managers, executives, and administrators who do not know how to conduct an efficient and effective meeting. What could often be achieved in 15 or 20 minutes drags on for an hour or more. Rambling and disorganized, these models of group waste sap organizations of millions of productive hours monthly and can even lead to a reduction in the creative problem-solving abilities and motivation of those who are forced to attend these "meatless meetings."

The surest way to guarantee highly productive meetings is to chair them (and to know what you're doing!). Unfortunately, we may not be the ones in charge and may have to delicately suggest ways to improve the productivity of meetings we attend. Regardless of who runs that next meeting, here are the secrets for a good one: Don't even call the meeting—unless it's the most efficient forum for achieving the objective. Would individual conversations be equally or more effective? Would a conference call be a viable option? Would a circulated memo do the trick? If a meeting *is* necessary, then . . .

➼ Publish an agenda and distribute it at least two days before the meeting. After each item listed on the agenda, enter an estimated time for discussion. This is a helpful psychological reminder for all the participants.

➼ Invite only those who are directly involved with the agenda items.

➼ Schedule a time and place that's convenient, and hold the meetings in a timely fashion, allowing an adequate response to the information or problem to be discussed.

➼ Inform attendees how long you expect the meeting to last and be a good "gatekeeper," i.e., stick to the agenda and don't let the discussions drag on past the point of productivity. One slick trick to control the length of meetings is to schedule them an hour before lunch or quitting time, which acts as an obvious stimulus to staying on track.

➼ Establish and maintain good interpersonal relations. Keep the climate relatively unstructured; encourage an open, uncritical exchange of ideas; and avoid preaching or pressuring.

➼ Pause at appropriate interim points to summarize progress on key issues.

➼ At the end of the meeting, state conclusions and actions to be taken. Assign responsibilities, taskings, and due dates.

➼ Publish minutes (if appropriate) and follow up on any taskings.

It's not difficult to run an effective meeting, and it doesn't require an above-average IQ. It merely takes some preplanning and disciplined control. If you're in charge, you can easily achieve success. If you're *not* in charge, the path to victory may be a bit more difficult since you'll have to deftly encourage those in control to improve the productivity of the meetings they chair.

• •

People who write the most interesting and effective letters never answer letters. They answer people.

—from Bits & Pieces

• •

CHAPTER 4

The Quill

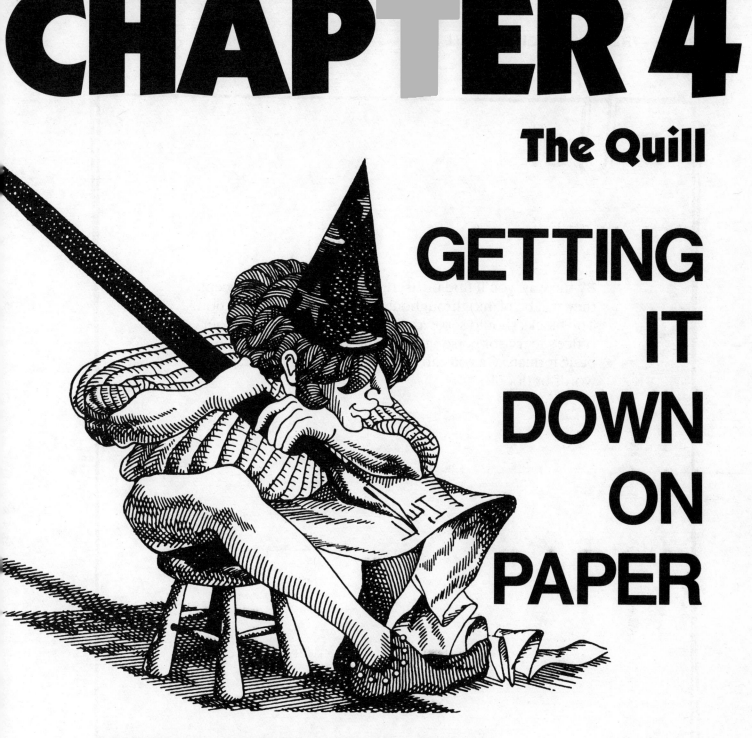

GETTING IT DOWN ON PAPER

FUNCTIONS AND FORMATS FOR WRITING

Letters, reports, and forms are the permanent life blood of all organizations. There are, quite literally, thousands of different formats. Fortunately, the *functions* of these many formats are very limited: to inform, to persuade, or to send a personal message of thanks, condolence, admonishment, etc. The purpose of the *T&Q* is to demystify the confusing thicket of formats and help you focus on the key functions and universal features of *all* correspondence.

If you can grasp the essential features of all written formats, then you'll be prepared to react successfully to any communications task that calls for writing. Let's begin.

P. S.

By the way, you'll find postscript blocks like these (except they will be blank) throughout the written formats section. The blocks should serve as mental compost piles for your office/supervisor/personal preference for changes to the basic formats. Or you can fill the spaces with disparaging words or doodles.

WHEN YOU WRITE FOR THE BOSS

Is there an added dimension when we write for the chairman of the board, the CEO, the COO, or the company president? From discussions with numerous senior officials and top-level executives, the answer is yes.

✍ Everything you read in this book about "analyze the purpose and audience" applies. Find out all you can about the boss' personal views on the subject and his or her relationship with the addressee. Try to capture the boss' wider perspective before you pick up your pen. What peripheral issues facing the boss could be directly or indirectly affected by your words? What is the desired purpose; what tone and style is most appropriate? If necessary, call the executive secretary or "chief of staff" and seek advice.

✍ Remember the ole KISS OFF—Keep It Simple, Silly, or Face Frustration. A boss' time is spread over many issues. Get to the point, make it, and move on. If the addressee needs only the time, don't send instructions on how to build a clock. Your first draft will probably be twice as long as it should be. If you must include details, use attachments or enclosures.

✍ Go easy on the modifiers. A boss doesn't need to say he or she is *very* interested in something—being interested is sufficient. Also, avoid emotionalism.

✍ *Be sure you're right.* From your logic to your grammar, from your facts and figures to your format, triple-check your work. You have nothing to lose but your credibility.

✍ Don't expect your glistening product to fly the first time. Not even the best staffers are clairvoyant.

Why should we write differently for senior executives? Why should that added dimension apply only to the boss? There's no good reason. We'd become better communicators if we assumed *all* of our correspondence were front-office bound.

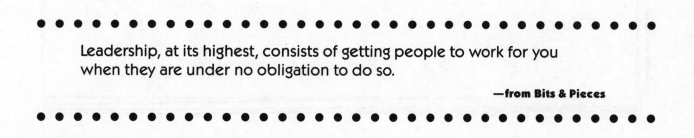

Leadership, at its highest, consists of getting people to work for you when they are under no obligation to do so.

—from Bits & Pieces

THE BUSINESS LETTER

KinderCare®

Kinder-Care Learning Centers, Inc. ● 2400 Presidents Drive ● P.O. Box 2151 ● Montgomery, Alabama 36197 ● (205) 277-5090

February 16, 1989

Ms. Susie Mahnke, Director
Kinder-Care Learning Center #1294
1197 Willis Ave.
Daytona Beach, FL 32014

Dear Susie,

Hats off to you and your staff for a fabulous grand opening this week at the Daytona Beach Community College Kinder-Care.

The center looked inviting, the program materials were apparent and the refreshment table appropriately commemorated Valentine's Day!

Thank you, too, for the king-sized Valentine card for Dr. Polk, the college president, presented by the children. He was delighted.

All of us from the corporate office felt welcome and proud of you, your staff and fellow directors who came to take our many guests on a center tour after the ribbon cutting. The media enjoyed the event and you are bound to get some good coverage.

I'm glad we had an opportunity to visit during the quiet time after the event. You are so knowledgeable about operating a successful center and I learned several things that will help our Communications Department support your work. Please keep us informed of your progress. I'm concerned that our partnership with DBCC will be fruitful for all of us.

Thank you again for making us feel so welcome. It was a very meaningful Valentine's Day!

Sincerely,

Ann Muscari, Vice President
Corporate Communications

pc: Allen Wankat, Region Manager
       Bill Castengara, District Manager

AM/sg

"For the Pre-school time of their lives"

THE BUSINESS LETTER

All letters "talk" to you in two ways. First, their *format* tells you if it's a business letter, a personal letter, a form letter, and/or whether or not it's coming from a person or company that takes pride in its work. A smudged letter full of errors says a lot, doesn't it? Secondly, the *content* tells you the sender's message. The first part of the *T&Q* prepared you to write clear and concise content; now we'll focus on acceptable formats.

Although there are hundreds of variations, nearly every business letter shares 10 common elements:

1. Letterhead/organization logo/address

2. Date when the letter was dispatched

3. Address of intended receiver as it will appear on the envelope

4. Salutation (usually "Dear Mr., Mrs., or Ms. Someone" unless the very formal "Dear Sir," "Dear Madam," or "Gentlemen" is more appropriate to the situation). When addressing a letter to an organization instead of an individual, use an attention line in place of the salutation; i.e., ATTENTION: Sales Department.

5. Body (the meat of your message)

6. Closing ("Sincerely," "Cordially," etc.)

7. Signature block includes signer's name and title

There's never time to do it right
but there's always time to do it over.

—**Mesikimen's Law**

8. Reference initials (signer's initials in caps, followed by a slash or colon and the preparer's initials in lower case)

9. Enclosure reminder (followed by a list of enclosures if there's more than one)

10. "PC" or "CC" notation (if anyone has been sent a personal or courtesy copy)

The precise location on the page of these 10 elements varies widely among organizations, and it would be a waste of your time and mine to include page after page of senseless examples (people actually get rich selling books that are full of that kind of trivia). It is of zero consequence to the well-being of the universe whether our business letters are full-blocked, blocked, semi-blocked, modified-blocked, or square-blocked; whether we use open, close, or standard punctuation; and whether we use oyster, saffron, or persimmon-colored paper. What matters is a pleasing-to-the-eye letter that's sincere and makes sense.

There are hundreds of different types of business letters, including letters of credit, reservation, orders, follow-up, confirmation, collection, inquiry, referral, remittance, complaint, claims, adjustment, invitation, litigation, sales, public relations, job offer, job termination, and bankruptcy, to name a few. Every bookstore contains a dozen or more books that give you explicit examples of how to write each type of letter. Don't waste your money. Since you've studied the six-step checklist you already know how to write any type of letter, and by relying on your own good sense and natural style, you'll be able to write business letters that sincerely speak to the reader.

Letters should be as brief as possible, but if you find it necessary to use a second page, use nonletterhead stationery. Your company or organization may have a standard format for official letters. If they don't, snoop around and find out what format is in vogue. If you're fortunate enough to be captain of your own commercial barge, you can create your own letterhead and format. In that case, I offer only one bit of advice—keep it simple.

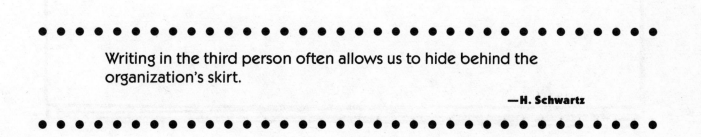

Writing in the third person often allows us to hide behind the organization's skirt.

—H. Schwartz

Kleinwaks/Rothco

P. S.

THE PERSONAL LETTER

3700 First Atlanta Tower
Atlanta, GA 30383

Telephone 404 658 1800

Price Waterhouse

December 14, 1987

Ms. Angela M. Humphreys
P.O. Drawer BX
University, Alabama 35486

Dear Angela:

I am delighted that you have chosen Price Waterhouse as
the place to begin your career in the business world.
I believe that you made the right decision.

I am sorry that we did not get to spend some time together
when I was visiting on December 8, 1987 but look forward
to visiting with you during my trips to The University
this spring.

Again, I look forward to working with you in the months
ahead. Good luck on your exams (I know you will do well)
and Merry Christmas!

Sincerely,

R. Wayne Jackson

RWJ/mfd

THE PERSONAL LETTER

The personal or social letter is more informal than the business letter and may or may not be on letterhead stationery. This type of communication was everyone's first experience at letter writing. You wrote these to your parents when you were away at Camp Runamuck, or maybe you had a pen pal in Australia. These letters are like phone calls on paper where the listener never talks.

A modern twist to this type of letter is the social business letter. This letter does not directly involve your company or organization, but it can build good will, which may ultimately affect the success of your company, product line, or political objective. Social business letters may include letters of condolence, appreciation, congratulations, announcement, invitation, etc.

Several format elements are common to personal or social business letters:

1. Letterhead/logo/address (optional)

2. Date

3. Salutation ("Dear _____")

4. Body

5. Closing ("Sincerely," or something more personal)

6. Signature (writing your name is sufficient, although some people sign above their typed name but use no title)

A well-crafted personal or social business letter is always good business and cannot fail to have a positive impact on your clients, customers, friends, or associates.

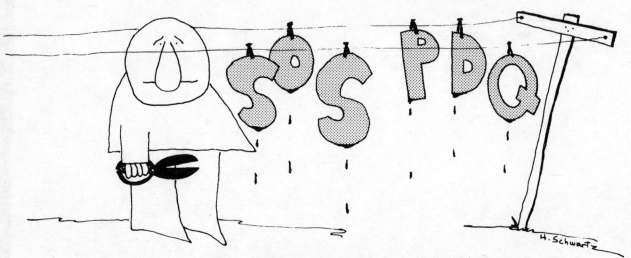

Are your memos cut and dried? Perhaps you need English that's *alive!*

(See pages 135-37 in the *T&Q*.)

THE MEMORANDUM

STAR CORP

MEMO

DATE: March 10, 1989

TO: Mr. Marks

FROM: Bobby Dunsmore

SUBJECT: Norcross Aviation Merger Package

I got a call from Seattle while you were out. Norcross Aviation wants a follow-up consultation on their merger package. Their CEO was impressed with the phase 1 work you did for them and particularly the cost data in Appendix 3 of STARCORP's report.

Put together an agenda for a follow-up visit and include a recommended executive training package. Contact at Norcross is still Bill Small. June-July is the desired timeframe, and see if Roberts can accompany you--we need to prepare her for eventual takeover of the Northeast Region.

rwd

SYSTEMS TECHNICAL ADVISORY & RESEARCH CORP.

P.O. Box 230146, Montgomery, Alabama 36123

(205) 244-1891

"*Reigned all day . . .*"

© *Clarence Brown. Reprinted by permission.*

P. S.

THE MEMORANDUM

Up to this point, you've been reading about formats primarily used to communicate with folks external to your organization. Internal communication, when it's not verbal, often takes the form of a memorandum, or memo. These are nothing more than notes to people who work together, and the only things that separate them from becoming letters are brevity, informality, and streamlined format.

Memos are generally quite brief—one or two paragraphs. Memos are also informal with organizational jargon/slang permitted. Regarding format, there are only five essential elements:

1. Date

2. To

3. From

4. Subject

5. Signature or initials at the end of the memo.

Authors of most "writing cookbooks" would like you to believe there are hints, secrets, or special principles for writing effective memos. Hogwash. A good memo contains the two elements found in any communication that could be considered good: clarity and brevity. Clarity means the reader knows who it's from and what action to take (is this for info only, or is a decision needed?). Clarity also means the content is logically organized and grammatically acceptable; brevity means the memo is no longer than it needs to be to get the message across.

Memos can be written on almost anything. Letterhead stationery is not used, but some organizations provide a standard memo form. Some of these preprinted formats include headings for the standard elements and a series of boxes that can be checked if the memo is for info, action, coordination, comment, etc. Other organizations allow employees to exercise their repressed creativity by producing or buying their own personalized memo pads, which can run the gamut from regal to raunchy and comic to clever. (Remember: no one has ever found a substitute for good taste.)

If your organization is insatiably high-tech, then paper memos are a thing of the past, and electronic mail is the standard. Even so, clarity and brevity remain the keys to successful memo writing.

● ●

We all know that simplicity. . . is close to the source.

—Dickey

● ●

P. S.

In the Royal Air Force we have to hand print all our messages. You'd be surprised how short they are. . . .

—WCDR David Wright

TELEGRAMS, MAILGRAMS, ETC.

HERB SCHWARTZ
3322 RIDGEFIELD DR
MONTGOMERY AL 36016 10AM

Western Union Mailgram ® UNITED STATES POSTAL SERVICE ® U.S.MAIL

4-033392S100 09/10/89 ICS IPMBNGZ NVFB
2052650737 MGMB TDBN MONTGOMERY-MM AL 26 09-10 0445P EST

▶ VICKI CHAMLEE, PRODUCTION MANAGER
PERGAMON-BRASSEY'S
8000 WEST PARK DR 4TH FL
MCCLEAN VA 22102

MANUSCRIPT SENT VIA FEDEX. GRAPHICS TO FOLLOW. ALERT LONDON. CHEERS.
   HERB SCHWARTZ

16:45 EST

MGMCOMP

Keep your head above water with a *read file*. This is a folder containing extra copies of letters, messages, and/or other documents used for periodic review by your office staff, for a cross-reference to the record copies filed in the same office, and for preparation of periodic reports.

Read file copies are maintained in chronological order and are destroyed 12 months after the monthly cutoff or when the purpose has been served, whichever is sooner.

TELEGRAMS, MAILGRAMS, ETC.

SUCCESS/FOUR FLIGHTS THURSDAY MORNING/ALL AGAINST TWENTY-ONE MILE WIND/STARTED FROM LEVEL WITH ENGINE POWER ALONE/AVERAGE SPEED THROUGH AIR THIRTY-ONE MILES/LONGEST FIFTY-NINE SECONDS/INFORM PRESS/HOME CHRISTMAS.

Telegram to the Rev. Milton Wright from Kitty Hawk, N.C.,
December 17, 1903

This curious category of correspondence refers to *any* form of written communication that carries a direct per-word or per-page cost. The only difference between these formats and others is the financial necessity to *edit out* all unnecessary words that are not critical to your intended message. Those who fancy themselves to be good editors view the telegram as the ultimate challenge!

After you have written that clear and concise message, go back and chop out every word that doesn't **have** to be there. Those who receive a telegram don't expect all the conventional niceties normally found in other communications, so you can dispense with the "dears," "pleases," and "thank yous." The 17-word sentence, "Please give us your order prior to June 1st so we can apply the 30 percent discount" becomes the six-word sentence, "Save 30 percent; order before June."

Many electronic message/mail companies have their own formats, forms, and rules so there's no point in wasting your time here with such enchanting things as which keyboard symbols are available and which are not (¢ vs. cents; @ vs. each, etc.). You might also become a fiscal fanatic, attempting to save money by compressing De Beers or Du Pont to DeBeers or DuPont, thus saving the cost of two words. Look at it this way: if you're that close to bankruptcy, you shouldn't have bought this book.

One final note about costs. You may recall that the first paragraph of this section mentioned *direct* per-word or per-page costs. This form of costing is not true of Federal Express, Purolator-Courier, telefaxing, datafaxing, etc. It is also not true of routine correspondence. *HOWEVER*, all words, in whatever form or format, cost somebody something, even though those costs may be sunk or indirect. So, once again, I bleat the plea to keep all of your communications clear and *brief*.

P. S.

Post Script

... added thought

If you're doing something the same way you have been doing it for
ten years, the chances are you are doing it wrong.

—Charles Kettering

THE BULLET BACKGROUND PAPER

BULLET BACKGROUND PAPER

ON

CAMPUS RECRUITING 1990-2000

The various law school deans have proposed a shift in philosophy for Trenton's future recruiting. This shift will be presented for open discussion at the next regents' meeting.

Thrust of the proposed shift:

- Expand recruiting to those students with 2.5 GPAs or higher rather than recruiting exclusively from 3.0 GPAs or higher.

- Change emphasis on LSAT scores/GPAs to 60 basis points from 80 basis points. Use the available 20 points for weighting of campus leadership activities.

  -- Weighting factors, suggested list of criteria, and administrative details have been worked out by ad hoc group led by Carlson.

- Rationale for change to policy based on 10-year analysis of graduating law students who typify the demographic makeup of our target population:

  -- Undergrad GPAs are less effective in determining graduate success than involvement in campus leadership activities.

    --- Some students take "gut course" majors (such as philosophy, religion, art) in order to build high GPAs for law school acceptance. Other students with more demanding majors (corporate finance, economics, engineering, math, biology) may have more potential but lower GPAs.

  -- Bar exams show gut course/high undergrad GPA students sustain 38 percent fail rate first time compared to 17 percent fail rates for moderate GPA students who carried tougher majors and who held campus leadership positions.

Although direct cause/effect relationship tenuous, shift in policy is probably warranted. Recommend gradual phase-in and comprehensive tracking.

Prof. Schwartz/Dean of Students/2445/sjm/August 15, 1990

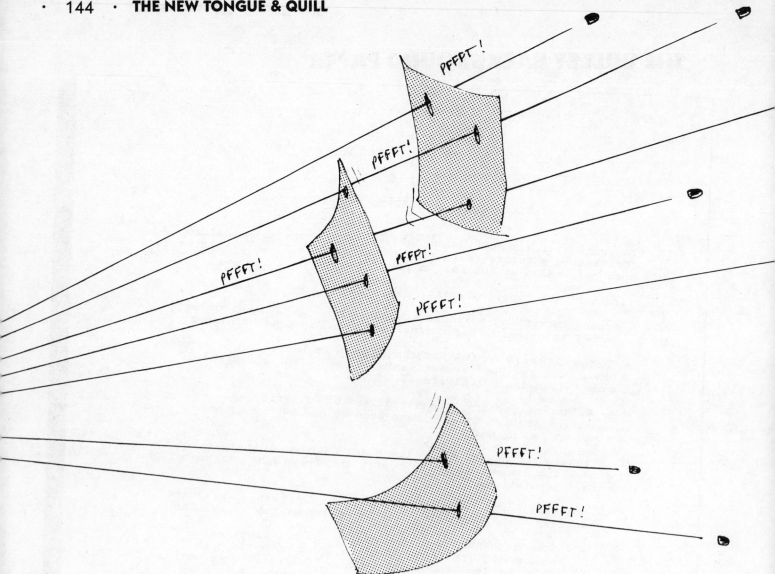

If the Ten Commandments had been written up as federal regulations and issued on stone, Moses would not have come down from Mount Sinai with two tablets. He would have come down with a hernia.

—**Jack Vosse, Lt. Col. USAF (Ret.)**

THE "BULLET" BACKGROUND PAPER

An increasingly popular format, borrowed from the U.S. military, is the "bullet" backgrounder. The bullet provides a concise, chronological evolution of a problem, a more complete summary of an information or decision package (in which case the bullet is attached to the package), or a more detailed explanation of what appears in an attached memo. The first paragraph of the bullet is used to identify the main thrust of the paper. Main ideas (which are not indented) follow the intro paragraph and may be as long as several sentences or as short as one word, for example, "Advantages." Secondary items follow a single dash, and tertiary items follow multiple indented dashes. Secondary or tertiary items can be as short as a few words or as long as a paragraph.

Format the bullet as you see on the preceding page. Center the heading on plain bond paper with 1-inch margins all around; single-space and block paragraphs, and double-space between items. Headings (such as SUBJECT, PROBLEM, BACKGROUND, DISCUSSION, CONCLUSION and/or RECOMMENDATION) are optional.

Bullet background papers may be longer than one page; however, their prime value is brevity achieved through a condensed format, absence of long transitions, and telegraphic wording.

Problems in developing backgrounders include:

- Too long (usually because writer did not analyze knowledge level of reader); main thoughts not emphasized.

- Additional support data not referenced by tab.

- If a document that supports the bullet is included in the package and tabbed, it should be mentioned in the bullet and the tab referenced (see page 167).

Bullet backgrounders should include an identification line (author's name, office symbol, phone number, typist's initials, computer document number, and date) at the lower left of the first page.

By permission of Johnny Hart and Creators Syndicate, Inc., 1989

P. S.

THE TALKING PAPER

TALKING PAPER

ON

CONTRACT VERSUS IN-HOUSE TRAINING

- The April conference will focus on cost benefits and long-term payback of contract and in-house training systems.

 -- Controller will present four comparative studies from like industries.

  --- Three of the four show increased effectiveness for in-house training of salesmen but not for technical specialists.

  --- Fourth study shows increased effectiveness for contract training of all personnel.

 -- Marketing and R&D will oppose contract training under any circumstances; they claim contractors can not react quickly enough to fast-breaking technology/policy/marketing changes.

- Our long-range planners will propose an orchestrated mix of methods. Key points to be made:

 -- Standard training elements (customer relations, product complaints, shipping, receiving, etc.,) can be contract on fixed-fee basis.

 -- In-house training will be best course for volatile areas such as tech services, new products marketing, installation, communications, etc.

- Impress on board members that degree of customer satisfaction is tough to measure in dollars, yet is ultimate payoff.

Ms. Lankoski/Strategic Planning/3281/mam/Apr 1, 90

Source of drawing unknown
Text by Schwartz

"Write as you speak" doesn't work if you talk funny.

—Joel Champion

TALKING PAPER

A talking paper is a concise document that provides either succinct comments for use during a meeting or information for decisionmakers on key points, facts, positions, or questions in a brief, orderly fashion. It can also be used as a memory tickler or quick reference outline. Like the bullet backgrounder, the talking paper originated in the U.S. military.

Format the talker to conform to the user's desires. It is normally prepared in short statement form using telegraphic wording. There is no standard format, but the example on the preceding page illustrates the most popular style. Headings, such as PURPOSE, DISCUSSION, RECOMMENDATION, are optional. Use a single dash before major thoughts and further indent subordinate thoughts; use the one-dash, two-dash, three-dash sequence. Single-space the talker (double-space between items) and limit it to one page when possible. Prepare a separate talker for every subject. Avoid extensive details and chronologies. If supporting information is needed, write a more detailed background paper to accompany the talking paper.

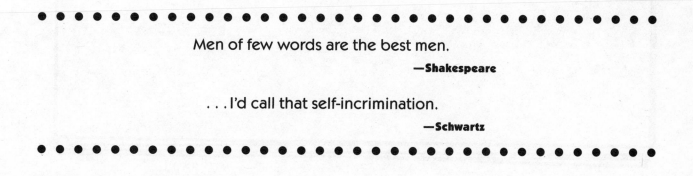

Men of few words are the best men.
—**Shakespeare**

. . . I'd call that self-incrimination.
—**Schwartz**

• •

Language not only affects the way we communicate, it also affects the way we think. Obscure, pretentious, wordy, indirect language obscures thought and fact. Use plain, ordinary English. Be economical with words. Use active voice. Avoid the language of overstatement.

—William G. Moore, Jr.

• •

P. S.

THE RÉSUMÉ

SUZIE CARLTON
115 Birch Street
Middletown, Iowa 52638
(516) 123-4567

SKILLS

Supervision/
Management

Supervised 2 enlisted personnel and 2 civilian employees in a U.S. Army Information Office. Manager of Chamber of Commerce Conventions Division. Supervised 9 employees who advertise/contract for convention business for the city. Responsible for $200,000 annual budget.

Editing/Writing

Edited and wrote articles for an 8-page monthly Army newsletter with a 6-state distribution list. Wrote articles for local newspaper/city magazines. Wrote ads designed to attract out-of-state conventions to the city.

Research

Designed survey instrument and collected responses from Army enlisted personnel in an 8-state area. Compiled results, analyzed data, and wrote final report for Army military personnel department.

EXPERIENCE

1985-Present   Writer-Editor, *Army Recruiting Journal*, Middletown, Iowa

1982-1985   Manager, Conventions Division, Middletown Area Chamber of Commerce

1980-1982   Editorial Assistant, Middletown News Agency

1971-1982   Volunteer, Tour Coordinator for Senior Citizen Group

1971-1979   Noncommissioned Officer (Staff Writer), Iowa National Guard

EDUCATION
B.S. in English, Troy State College, Middletown, Ohio, 1980

Enrolled in Master's Program, Troy State College

PERSONAL DATA
Married; 3 children
Hobbies: Art collecting, jogging, ballroom dancing

"*I'm so sorry you've been inconvenienced, Wotan.
I just naturally thought when I said 'God' that I
would get—you know—Jehovah.*"

Drawing by J. B. Handelsman; © 1974 *The New Yorker Magazine, Inc.*

THE RÉSUMÉ

When you are vying for a job, it will be to your benefit, no matter what your position, to prepare a résumé of your work experience, special qualifications, and education. Many times your résumé will be the first impression a potential employer has of *you*. That means that the way it is written and how it looks are a direct reflection of *you* and your communication and organization ability.

WHAT FORMAT?

The format you choose depends upon the specific reason you need the résumé (a "feeler" to send to multiple companies, a response to a particular job announcement, a request from a particular person, etc.). The following are some of the choices.

Chronological résumé: An outline of your work experience, periods of employment, and education (in reverse order—most recent information first). Stresses your major responsibilities, but does not concentrate on your accomplishments, skills, or potential. Used mostly by those people who have been steadily employed, and their current experience is applicable to the position they are seeking.

Functional résumé: Provides a career/job objective statement, and allows you to emphasize your abilities, accomplishments, and potential by grouping them into functional areas (training, sales, procurement, accounting, etc.). The functional résumé also allows you to include related experience gained through volunteer work or other nonpaid means. The functional résumé is used mostly by people who are not currently working in the occupation or profession they are trying to enter.

Combination chronological/functional résumé: Combines a chronological history of your work experience and a list of your areas of expertise (see sample on previous page). This résumé is a popular choice because it allows you to cover a wider variety of subjects/ qualifications and is ideal for those who are trying to reenter the job market or change careers.

Targeted résumé: As its name implies, this résumé is written for a *targeted* position. Its main entries should be a statement of your capabilities, achievements, experience, and education that are directly related to the targeted position.

· ·

The closest most people ever come to reaching their ideal is when they write their résumés.

anonymous

· ·

THINGS TO INCLUDE

As a minimum, include the following:

Name, address, and phone number (including the area code) on the top of the first page.

Work experience, periods of employment, and job titles (include military assignments if relevant). List (in reverse chronological order) periods of employment (or military assignments), expanding on the scope and responsibilities of those positions that are most relevant to the position you are seeking.

Education. List your education in reverse chronological order. Begin with your highest degree, and list the degree, institution, location, and year graduated. Include education/ training acquired during military service or through workshops, seminars, and continuing education classes that is relevant to the position you are seeking.

Personal data. Such things as marital status, children, hobbies, and health should be included. If in doubt, leave this category off your résumé.

WHAT ELSE?

The following are suggested topics you may want to consider including in your résumé. Choose only those pertinent to the job you are seeking, or add topics of your own choosing that you feel might encourage a potential employer to interview you. A word of caution: more is not necessarily better. You don't want your résumé so loaded and long that a potential employer would be inclined to throw it in the trash before reading it.

- Summary of qualifications (if seeking a particular job)

- Introduction or job objective (most often put in cover letter)

- Qualifications, special skills or capabilities

- Career accomplishments

- Languages

- Honors, awards, achievements

- Military service

- Professional development, affiliations

- Hobbies or personal interests

- References (use only if requested by potential employer)

- Memberships

- Credentials, licenses

DON'T INCLUDE

- Photograph

- Salary information

- Age

- Religious affiliation

- Irrelevant or negative information

IN SUMMARY

Take the time to prepare your résumé properly or invest the money to have a professional prepare it for you. Put a lot of thought into it, and have someone you trust read it and give you an honest opinion. Use action words to begin your sentences ("wrote," "taught," "reviewed," "supervised," "developed," "updated," "revised," etc.); be consistent in your use of underlines, indentations, and capital letters; write it in plain language; and make sure it is neat, uncluttered, and accurate. It must be long enough to cover relevant information but brief enough so as not to bore a potential employer (two pages max!). Have your résumé typed on good quality, white or off-white paper, *and it must be error free*. Choose the format that will work to your best advantage. Mix formats if doing so will show you in the best light! Update your résumé when necessary, but *never* update it with handwritten notes. Always give a potential employer a clean, unmarked original or good photocopy.

COVER LETTER

A cover letter should always accompany your résumé. It should be addressed to a specific person and contain information that will encourage that person to read the attached résumé and want to interview you. It should be typed on 8½- x 11-inch, good quality, white or off-white paper (never handwritten) and should not exceed one page. The last paragraph should ask for a meeting and say that you will follow up at a later time/date.

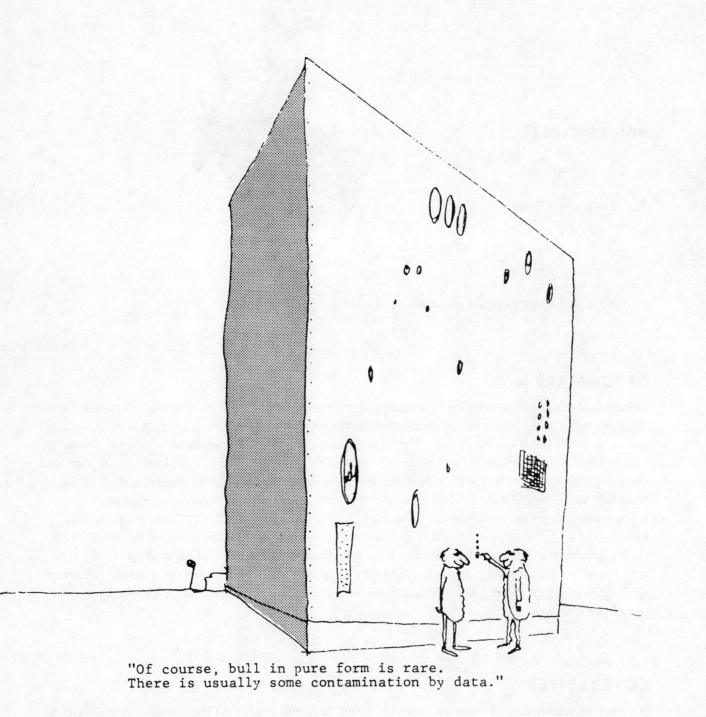

"Of course, bull in pure form is rare.
There is usually some contamination by data."

N. A. Valencia (by permission)

CHAPTER 5
Solving Problems on Paper

. . .OR EVERYTHING YOU WERE AFRAID SOMEONE WOULD EVENTUALLY TELL YOU ABOUT PROBLEM-SOLUTION REPORTING.

STUDIES, REPORTS, AND PROPOSALS

Studies, reports, and proposals are three words (among others) that we often use interchangeably to refer to documents (thick or thin) that update, investigate, and/or recommend. They can be

- Formal: Written in the third person with extensive use of passive voice.

- Informal: Written using "I" or "we" with extensive use of active voice.

- Prescribed Format: Using specific instructions for typographic format, topic/section/paragraph headings, length, and/or routing/number of copies.

- Open Format: Your choice! Good sense and good taste apply. I'd suggest wide margins all around (1½-inch), printing on one side of the page only, and a graphically appealing cover/binder. Check the office files or the front office to find out what formats have been used in successful reports. No use reinventing a wheel that already rolls smoothly!

Reports (and I'll use that term to apply to studies and proposals as well) can be as glitzy and photo-filled as an AT&T annual report to stockholders or as simple as a three-page black-on-white suggestion that you make to your boss about some relatively esoteric idea you've been fumbling with.

PROBLEM-SOLUTION REPORTING

The most challenging type of report involves some form of problem solution reporting, and that's the focus of this section. (Nobody needs detailed help on how to develop a simple informational report—it's no more complex than a business letter.)

Problem-solution reports expose a specific *thought process*, and they demand very careful preparation and organization. There is a limitless array of procedures and formats, but the approach I'll explain here provides *all of the key features* you'll find in any report that aims to solve a problem.

There is always an easy solution to every human problem—neat, plausible, and wrong.

—H.L. Mencken

ACTIONS PRIOR TO WRITING YOUR REPORT

Before you can report on a problem, you must mentally solve it. Here's a logical sequence of essential elements:

1. Analyze the audience. You usually solve problems dropped on you by the hierarchy. Sometimes you generate your own areas or subjects that call for analysis. In any case, there will be political and operational constraints that affect your problem-solving process. Do some reflective thinking about the environment you're operating in.

2. Limit the problem. Restrict it to manageable size by fixing the who, what, when, why, and how of the situation. Eliminate unnecessary concerns. Narrow the problem statement to exactly what you will be discussing; a common error is a fuzzy or inaccurate problem statement. For example, if the problem is the use of amphetamines and barbiturates among employees, the problem statement "To reduce the crime rate of Ace, Inc." would be too broad. So would "How to detect and limit the use of dangerous drugs at Ace, Inc." More to the point would be "To detect and eliminate the causes of amphetamine and barbiturate usage among the employees of Ace, Inc."

The problem should eventually be stated in one of three ways:

> *As a question:*
> What should we do to detect and eliminate the causes of amphetamine and barbiturate usage among our employees at Ace, Inc.?

> *As a statement of need or purpose:*
> Ace, Inc. needs to develop ways to detect and eliminate the. . . .

> *As an infinitive phrase:*
> To detect and eliminate the causes. . . .

3. Analyze the whole problem. Do the parts suggest other problems that need separate handling? Or do the parts relate so closely to the whole situation that you need only one approach?

4. Gather data. Collect all information pertinent to the problem. (Tips on how and where to conduct staff research can be found in "Conduct the Research" section.)

5. Evaluate your information. Is the information from reliable witnesses? Is it from qualified authorities? Does it qualify as solid support?

● ●

The real mark of the creative person is that the unforeseen problem is a joy and not a curse.

—Mackworth

● ●

6. Organize your information. One way to organize information is to place it under headings titled facts, assumptions, and criteria.

Facts should be just that, not opinions or assertions. Identify only those facts that directly bear on the problem.

Assumptions are important because they are always necessary. To reduce a research project to manageable size, it is usually necessary to accept certain things as being true, even if you are not absolutely sure they are. The validity of your assumptions usually has a great deal to do with the validity of your conclusion. Sometimes, desired conclusions can be supported with certain unrealistic assumptions. In evaluating research, you should seek out the assumptions and make some judgment as to how reasonable they are. If you feel the assumptions are unrealistic, you should make whatever assumptions you feel are correct and try to judge the effect of these assumptions on the conclusions of the study. Sometimes a lovely and logical study explodes in the face of the writer because the assumptions were incredibly weak or simply unsupportable.

Criteria are those standards, requirements, or limitations used to test possible solutions. The criteria for a problem solution are sometimes provided in complete form by your boss when you are assigned the problem. Sometimes, criteria are inherent in the nature of the obstacle causing the problem. The obstacle can only be overcome within certain physical limits, and these limits will establish the criteria for the problem solution. In most cases, however, criteria are usually inherent in your own frame of reference and in the goal you are trying to attain. This goal and this frame of reference will tolerate only certain problem solutions, and the limits of this tolerance will establish the criteria for the problem solution.

Remember this: *the criteria will not be very useful if you cannot clearly test the possible solutions against them!* Since weak or even lousy criteria are often seen in problem-solution reports, let's examine three examples of criteria and assess their value:

1. "The total solution must not cost more than $60,000 annually."

2. "The solution must result in a 25 percent increase in sales."

3. "The solution must be consistent with the boss' philosophy on personnel management."

Criterion 1 is fine; you could easily test your proposed solutions against a specific cost. Criterion 2 looks good on the surface, but sales rates result from numerous and complex variables. You probably could not guarantee the decisionmaker that your solution would lead to a 25 percent increase. It might improve the rate of sales or actually lead to a rate higher than 25 percent, but before your boss actually

• •

A problem well stated is a problem half solved.

—Charles Kettering

• •

implements your solution, how would you know that? If a criterion cannot be used to test solutions before implementation, it is not an acceptable criterion. Criterion 3 isn't bad, but it's fuzzy. Perhaps it could be written more precisely or left off the formal report altogether. You could still use it intuitively to check your solutions, but realize that when you use hidden criteria, your report will be less objective.

7. List possible solutions. Approach the task of creating solutions with an open mind. Develop as many solutions as possible.

8. Test possible solutions. Test each solution by using criteria formed while gathering data. Weigh one solution against another after testing each. Be sensitive to your personal biases and prejudices. Strive for professional objectivity.

9. Select final solution. Select the best possible solution—or a combination of the best solutions—to fit the situation. Most problem solutions fall into one of the three patterns listed below. Do not try to force your report into one of these patterns if it doesn't appear to fit.

Single best possible solution. This one is basic and the most commonly used. You select the best solution from several possible ones.

Combination of possible solutions. You may need to combine two or more possible solutions for your best possible solution.

Single possible solution. At times, you may want to report on only one possible solution.

"HERB HAS REALLY BEEN IN A RUT LATELY..."

The obscure we see eventually, the completely apparent takes longer.
—**Edward R. Murrow**

10. Act. Jot down the actions required for the final solution. Your comments here will eventually lead to the specific action(s) your boss should take to implement the solution (this will eventually appear in the "Action Recommended" section when you write up the report). If there is no implementing document for the decisionmaker to sign, you need to state clearly other specific action the boss must take to implement your proposal. No problem is complete until action has been planned and executed.

NOTE: In actual practice, the steps of problem solving do not always follow a definite and orderly sequence. The steps may overlap, more than one step may be considered at one time, or developments at one step may cause you to reconsider a previous step. For example, the data you collect may force you to redefine your problem. Similarly, while testing solutions, you may think of a new solution, or, in the process of selecting a final solution, you may discover you need additional information. The steps just outlined can serve as a checklist to bring order to your mental processes.

WRITING YOUR REPORT

Here is an all-purpose format prototype for a problem-solution report. Use only those portions of this format necessary for your particular report. If you omit certain paragraphs, renumber subsequent paragraphs accordingly.

FROM: (You or your title/office symbol, etc.)   (Date)

SUBJECT: Proposed Solution for the XYZ Problem

TO: (Your decisionmaker)

PROBLEM

1.   (Clear, brief statement of the problem)

FACTORS BEARING ON THE PROBLEM

2.   Facts.

     a. . . . .

     b. . . . .

3.   Assumptions.

4.   Criteria.

5.   Definitions.

DISCUSSION

6. . . . .

CONCLUSION

7. . . . .

ACTION RECOMMENDED

8. . . . .

(Your name/title)   Enc. (if appropriate)

By now you probably realize the problem-solution report is a record that presents data collected, discusses possible solutions to the problem, and indicates the best solution. It is not a form for solving a problem. You should mentally solve your problem first and then report the solution in writing. The format of the report includes a heading, a body, an ending, and, when necessary, enclosures.

Heading. After the FROM caption, enter your office symbol; if appropriate, add your name. After the SUBJECT caption, state the report subject as briefly and concisely as possible. However, use a few extra words if this will add meaning to your subject. After the TO caption, enter the name and/or office symbol of the decisionmaker or individual who is to receive your report.

Body. The body of the report contains five parts: (1) Problem, (2) Factors Bearing on the Problem, (3) Discussion, (4) Conclusion, and (5) Action Recommended. These parts coincide with the steps of problem solving.

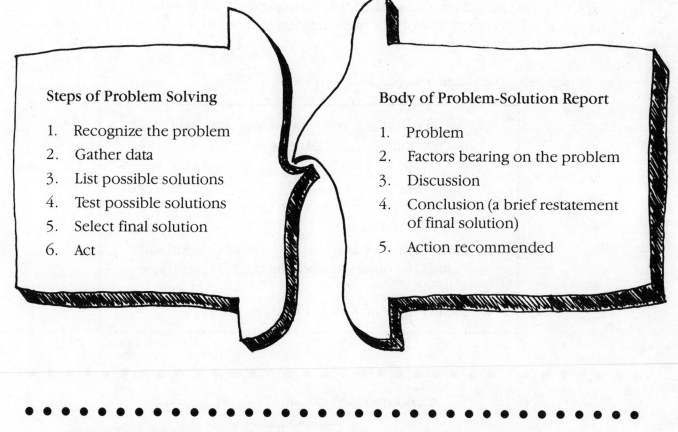

Steps of Problem Solving

1. Recognize the problem
2. Gather data
3. List possible solutions
4. Test possible solutions
5. Select final solution
6. Act

Body of Problem-Solution Report

1. Problem
2. Factors bearing on the problem
3. Discussion
4. Conclusion (a brief restatement of final solution)
5. Action recommended

There are in fact two things, science and opinion; the former begets knowledge, the latter ignorance.

—Hippocrates

- **Problem.** The statement of the problem tells the reader what you are trying to solve. No discussion is necessary at this point; a simple statement of the problem is sufficient. You have sufficient opportunity to discuss all aspects of the problem later in the report.

- **Factors bearing on the problem.** This part contains the facts, assumptions, criteria, and definitions you used to build possible solutions to your problem. Devote separate paragraphs to facts, assumptions, criteria, and definitions as shown in the sample study report. Obviously, if you write a report in which you have no assumptions or definitions, omit either or both. Include only those important factors you used to solve your problem. Briefly state whatever you include. Put lengthy support material in attachments. Write each sentence completely enough that you don't force the reader to refer to the enclosures to understand what you've written. Maintain your thought sequence throughout the body of the report.

- **Discussion.** This part of the report is crucial because it shows the logic used in solving the problem. Generally, some background information is necessary to properly introduce your problem. The introduction may be only one paragraph, but it could contain several paragraphs, depending on the detail required. Once the intro is complete, use one of the following outlines to discuss your thought process.

When using the single best possible solution,

1. List all possible solutions that you think will interest the decisionmaker.

2. Show how you tested each possible solution against the criteria, listing both the advantages and disadvantages. Use the same criteria to test each possible solution.

3. Show how you weighed each possible solution against the others in selecting the best possible solution.

4. Clearly indicate the best possible solution.

● ●

Intentions don't count!
—Jean-Paul Sartre

. . . neither does second place!
—Herb-Jacques Schwartz

● ●

When using the combination of possible solutions,

1. List all the possible solutions that you think will interest the decisionmaker.

2. Show how you tested each possible solution against the criteria, listing both advantages and disadvantages. Use the same criteria to test each possible solution.

3. Show how you weighed each possible solution against the other possible solutions and why you retained certain ones as a partial solution to the problem.

4. Show how and why you combined the retained possible solutions.

When using the single possible solution,

1. List your single solution.

2. Test it against the criteria.

3. Show how and why this solution will solve the problem.

NOTE

No matter how you organize your report, these points are important:

- Make it brief
- Maintain a sequence of thought throughout
- Show the reader how you reasoned the problem through
- Use enclosures for support, but include enough information in the body of the report to make sense without referring to the enclosures

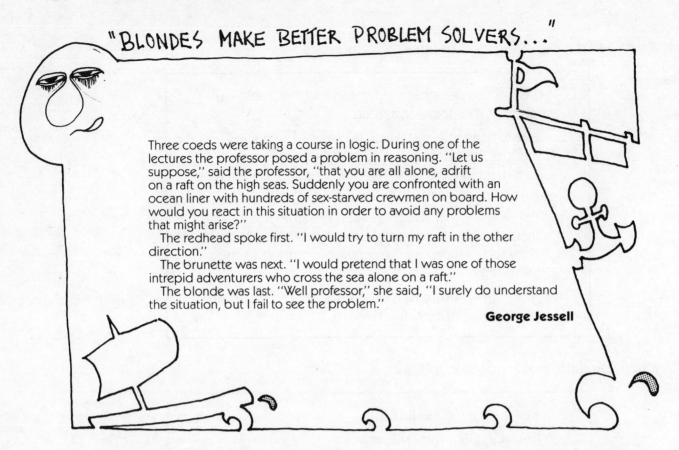

"BLONDES MAKE BETTER PROBLEM SOLVERS..."

Three coeds were taking a course in logic. During one of the lectures the professor posed a problem in reasoning. "Let us suppose," said the professor, "that you are all alone, adrift on a raft on the high seas. Suddenly you are confronted with an ocean liner with hundreds of sex-starved crewmen on board. How would you react in this situation in order to avoid any problems that might arise?"

The redhead spoke first. "I would try to turn my raft in the other direction."

The brunette was next. "I would pretend that I was one of those intrepid adventurers who cross the sea alone on a raft."

The blonde was last. "Well professor," she said, "I surely do understand the situation, but I fail to see the problem."

George Jessell

- **Conclusion.** After showing how you reasoned the problem through, state your conclusion. The conclusion must provide a complete, workable solution to the problem. The conclusion is nothing more than a brief restatement of the best possible solution or solutions. The conclusion must not continue the discussion. It should completely satisfy the requirements of the problem; it should never introduce raw material.

- **Action recommended.** This part tells the reader what action is necessary. The number of recommendations is not important; just be sure you have "completed staff work."

Word the recommendations so your boss need only sign them into action. Do not recommend alternatives. This does not mean you cannot consider alternative solutions under "Discussion." It means that, in recommending action, you commit yourself to the line of action you judge best. That's what you're getting paid for!

You must relieve the decisionmaker of the research and study necessary to decide among several alternatives. Give precise guidance on what you want the decisionmaker to do; i.e., "Sign the implementing letter at Enclosure 1." (Normally, implementing documents should be the first enclosure.) Don't submit a rubber turkey; recommendations like "Recommend further study" or "Either solution A or B should be implemented" indicate the decisionmaker picked the wrong person to do the study.

Ending. Follow the format shown on the sample report. The ending contains the name and title of the person or persons responsible for the report and a listing of enclosures.

Enclosures. Since the body of the report must be brief, relegate as much of the detail as possible to the enclosures. For example,

- Include, as enclosures, the directives, policy letters, etc., necessary to support the recommended actions.

- The body may reference the authority directing the study. An enclosure may contain an actual copy of the directive, memo, etc.

- The body may contain an extract or a condensed version of a quote. An enclosure may contain a copy of the complete quote.

- The body may contain a statement that requires support. An enclosure may state the source and include the material that verifies that statement.

- The body may refer to a chart or information contained in a chart. An enclosure may include the complete chart. (Design the chart to fit the overall proportions of the report or fold the chart to fit these proportions.)

- If directives or detailed instructions are required to implement the recommended action, include drafts of them as enclosures.

NOTE: Although seldom required, identify material needed to support an enclosure as an appendix to the enclosure.

Tabs. Number tabs (paper or plastic indicator) to help the reader locate enclosures or appendices. Affix each tab to a blank sheet of paper and insert immediately preceding the enclosure. If it is not practical to extract the supporting material from a long or complex document used as an enclosure, affix the tab to that page within the enclosure or appendix where the supporting material is located.

Position the tab for Enclosure 1 to the lower right corner of a sheet of paper. Position the tab for each succeeding enclosure slightly higher on a separate sheet so that all the tabs can be seen.

Completed staff work. A problem-solution report should represent completed staff work. This means that you have solved a problem and presented a complete solution to the boss. The solution should be complete enough that the decisionmaker has only to approve or disapprove.

The impulse to ask the chief what to do occurs more often when the problem is difficult. This impulse often comes to the inexperienced employee frustrated over a hard job. It's easy to ask the chief what to do, and it appears easy for the chief to answer. But you should resist that impulse. Your job is to advise your boss what should be done—provide answers, not questions. Of course, it's all right to inquire at any point in the problem-solving procedure if you need to find out whether you are on the right track. This coordination often saves untold hours.

Some final thoughts on completed staff work and problem-solution reporting:

✔ Make sure your staff work is complete. This protects your boss from half-baked ideas, voluminous written reports, and immature oral explanations. It also allows the decisionmaker more time to do the things that only he or she can do.

✔ Unleash your latent creativity! Completed staff work provides the creative staff worker a better chance to get a hearing.

✔ Schedule time to work the problem. Most problems worthy of analysis require considerable study and reflection for most folks.

✔ Avoid simplistic solutions. There's usually no hidden cause that will jump up and bite your kneecap; e.g., "Fire the idiots and get on with the program."

✔ Don't assume that the heavier and fancier the study, the better it is. A smart decisionmaker focuses on the relevance and accuracy of your supporting material and the logic of your argument.

✔ Don't develop a study in isolation. If you point the finger at someone or some department, or if your solution requires a change in someone's operation, you'd better get a reaction from such people before you drop the bomb. They can make you look mighty foolish if you find out later they were operating under a constraint you were unaware of. Your boss may end up shoveling it, and you'll end up eating it.

✔ Remember the final test for completed staff work: if you were the boss, would you be willing to stake your professional reputation or the future economic health of your organization on this problem-solution report? If the answer is no, go back to "Go." Do not collect $200. It's time to start over.

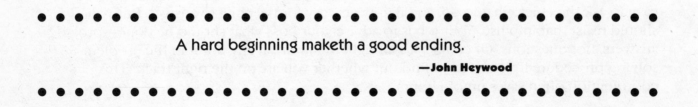

A hard beginning maketh a good ending.

—John Heywood

THE COORDINATION GAME

Every large organization has its own procedures for processing paperwork. In most cases, there is some formal (or informal) method used to move new ideas/solutions/proposals through the organization to get the opinions of key players. This process is known variously as "staffing," "reviewing," "chopping," "coordinating," etc. As you see from the title of this section, I prefer the term "coordination."

A coordinated paper tells the decisionmaker that it represents the best course of action and includes the views of all people interested in the subject. Coordination also tells the decisionmaker that the people who coordinated agree to support the position stated in the paper and to take subsequent actions within their responsibilities. Those two sentences describe good coordination. However, even at best, it's a very squirrelly game.

Like riding a bicycle, there's not much use in reading a manual on how to do it. Coordinating can't be taught by a checklist anymore than you can achieve balance on a bicycle by listening to a lecture. But training wheels and traffic rules can ease the inescapable process of "getting on and falling off." Here are several aids that may reduce your bruises when you peddle your paperwork through the maze.

• •

Great discoveries and improvements invariably involve the cooperation of many minds.

—Alexander Graham Bell

• •

PICKING YOUR "KNOWS"

As soon as you unpack your office supplies and join a new staff, look through the organization's telephone directory. Whom do you know? Call them; make initial contact; find out what their act is and what gears they grease in the mechanism. If it's a huge gaggle, like IBM, forget the telephone book trick. Instead, look around for familiar faces. Build a network of knowledgeables. This is smart personal relations, and you can benefit each other; good contacts are worth their weight in aspirin. They can assist you in coordinating your paperwork through their branch, division, department, or whatever. And they'll expect the same from you when they're running the gauntlet. In building your network, don't forget to check the old heads in your own office area; they know the contacts and can often steer you in the right direction.

PRIDE GOETH BEFORE A FALL

Pride of authorship is almost instinctive; at least some people's behavior would lead you to that conclusion. Admittedly, it's tough to be the Gingerbread Man with everyone taking a bite of your cookie, but that's life. The editorial comments of other people can improve most of our writing and, sometimes, our logic. When you coordinate paperwork, you should expect modifications in your personal prose and changes in the basic content. The wisest approach is to allow another person to chop on your work well before you begin to coordinate.

THE GODFATHERS

Many organizations have an underground of expertise that operates at your level. This underground is highly developed in many organizations. These people will pass judgment on your package. They know what their bosses will buy and what they won't buy. They know solid rock from thin ice. They know who needs to chop on your project. In other words, knowing them and working with them are down payments against hypertension.

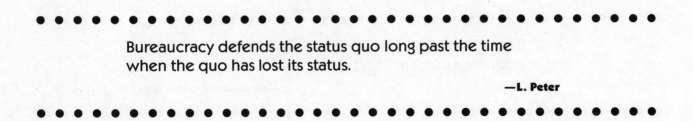

> Bureaucracy defends the status quo long past the time when the quo has lost its status.
>
> **—L. Peter**

On large staffs, the executive secretary, in most cases, is the key to the underground and can tip you off on who's who. Work this subterranean network before you go public. The hurdles will be lower, your successes will be greater, and you will be less likely to take a hit when you surface.

THE BOSS SAYS...

A lot of rancid peanut butter has been palmed off with that line. Who says the boss said it? In what context? Prove it. How do you *know* what he or she thinks? No doubt you've heard of the parlor game in which A tells B a story and then B repeats it to C; by the time F brings the tale back to A, Herbert was infatuated with *Malcom* instead of Marge. . . .

Some folks who should know better get suckered on "The boss says. . ." or "I heard the VP wants . . . ." These phrases have been known to generate massive amounts of staff rubbish by good people who were reluctant to confirm secondhand stories. Don't chicken out; *check* it out.

IF YOU WROTE IT, RIDE IT

This should be obvious, but many folks have temporarily lost their paperwork because they either didn't hand carry it or didn't buttonhole someone in the coordinating office to call when it was ready for pick up. Remember the famous Shakespearean verse: "Here lie the bones of Mr. Jones who put his package in distribution. . . ." No one needs the embarrassment of not being able to put their hands on their staff work. Don't construe this to mean everything must be hand carried—that's neither reasonable nor necessary. Secretaries in the coordinating offices can keep an eye on your staff work, and your contacts can also act as package monitors. The point is, know where your paperwork packages are.

HOW MANY IS ENOUGH?

Coordinating or deciding **who** will coordinate doesn't occur in a vacuum. Normally, by the time a task floats down to you, memos, notes, and other bits and pieces glued to the instructions will give you a pretty good idea of whom to coordinate with and whom to avoid. Also, during the coordination process you'll get more suggestions for coordination. If you receive no guidance, make your best guess. The process itself will add any missed offices.

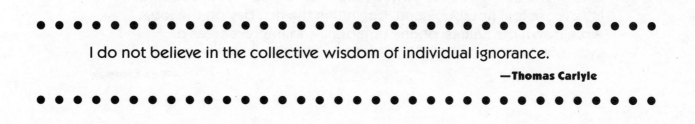

I do not believe in the collective wisdom of individual ignorance.

—**Thomas Carlyle**

BUMP THE HEAVY FIRST

Almost every project or problem tackled by a staff member (that's you!) involves a "heavy"—an individual who swings more clout than anyone else. "Heavy" can mean heavy in rank, heavy in expertise or concern, or heavy in the informal chain. If you can win the concurrence of your heavy early in the coordination process, other folks will tend to fall in line. Conversely, nonconcurrence from a heavy can put a sizeable hole below your waterline. Keep in mind that your heavy may change from problem to problem. One final comment: don't ruin your whole coordination day with a breach of protocol; make sure you know the heavies who don't mind coordinating before some of the lesser peons.

DEADLINE ETIQUETTE

In sending out packages for coordination, be careful not to demand action of an office or agency higher than your own. This doesn't mean that you can't tip the secretary or one of your contacts that the package is "supposed to be in the front office by Friday." This will inform them of *your* deadline, and it should encourage them to move the package through their office with appropriate speed.

BUSTING A DEADLINE

Ask for an extension if you must, but don't *ever* fail to meet an assigned deadline. That's a definite no-no.

SHOTGUN STAFFING

Prepare many copies of the package and give one to all interested agencies simultaneously. Your contacts can usually serve as goatherders for the package during its stay in their head shepherd's office. This speeds the coordination process, especially when nonconcurrences or suggested changes are minimal. Shotgun staffing is most useful when time is tight.

EARLY BIRDS GET RID OF THE WORMS

Another time saver when you're haunting the halls is to give a *draft* package to potential coordinators and contacts. This will allow them time to study the issue and make inputs to the final product. It will save time when you come around to coordinate formally.

• •

One of the best pieces of advice I ever heard was, "Get yourself a little loose-leaf notebook and, beginning the first day on the job, write down the names, phone numbers, and interest areas of everyone you contact." I did. It's been a three-ring life saver.

—**Don Kaufman**

• •

MA BELL CAN HELP YOU MAKE IT HAPPEN

Coordination by telephone is not always possible, but when you can use the telephone, don't hesitate. Doing the job with the least amount of muss and fuss is the name of the game. You can coordinate some small, fairly routine packages entirely by telephone. Even when you have a particularly complex package that may require coordination with 30 to 40 people, you may be able to telecoordinate with those folks who are well "inside" the package and are totally familiar with it.

Telecommunications can also help ensure that the heavy hitters are available to coordinate. Checking before you charge off can save needless trips up and down the halls, and it can prevent lonely hours in the outer office waiting, and waiting, and waiting. One last thought before we hang up: when *you* are tapped to coordinate over the phone, be sure to ask if there are any nonconcurrences. Maybe you're being asked to coordinate on a package no one else likes. Although this is no reason *not* to coordinate, you owe it to yourself to get as complete a picture of the package as possible. Always ask specific questions. It's fine to trust your fellow workers when they call, but cut the cards.

IF AT FIRST YOU DON'T SUCCEED...

Occasionally, no matter how well you've built the package or how carefully you've planned coordination, you'll hear these saddest of words, "I can't agree on this." You can now change your package to accommodate the opposing view or press on with a nonconcurrence attached. However, since writing a nonconcurrence takes time for the person who balks, you can sometimes swing a concurrence if you're persuasive and determined. Another alternative is to make minor concessions that don't change the thrust of your report but satisfy the potential noncoordinator. On the other hand, a nonconcurrence attached to your package may not be all bad. It depends on what it contains and, perhaps more important, on who nonconcurred. If your stock is higher, the nonconcurrence could conceivably help further coordination. Generally, it's best to float an action with total staff concurrence. However, controversial issues can't always be resolved except at a high level. Providing a framework for decisionmaking is a major function of the organization and your staff work.

• •

People who believe that the dead never come back to life should visit this place at quitting time.

—an anonymous employee of a Fortune 500 company

• •

ON ARCHING YOUR BACK

Don't waste emotional ammo on the irrelevant; a compromise position may be necessary when you are coordinating. But, once in a while, you may have to dust off the tubes of war paint, apply generously, plant your feet firmly, and unload both barrels.

Some crazies out there will never see the logic of your labor. Enlightenment forever eludes their intellectual grasp. However, arch your back when you can't fully support your views, and no one will eulogize your passing.

OH, OH, HERE IT COMES...

Although I stated earlier that you can't learn how to coordinate using a checklist, I've slipped one in anyway. Don't get too excited. It's no assurance against getting your tongue stuck in the toaster, but along with the preceding tips, the checklist may help you to recall something that might otherwise slip by. Just follow the finger.

Remember: Good coordinating, like effective writing and speaking, is tough work and improves only with lots of practice. The purpose of coordination is to put the "corporate stamp" on your package. If you view coordination as an unnecessary bureaucratic hassle that undermines your work, you're headed for trouble. On the other hand, if you believe your organization will have a better product because you were smart enough to coordinate properly and get help from lots of folks, then you're on the right airline. Good luck and fast peddling!

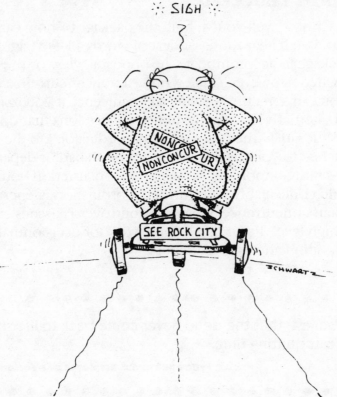

COORDINATOR'S CHECKLIST

☐ Before requesting formal coordination from others, determine the position your office will take. If necessary,
- Check pertinent background information.
- Seek your supervisor's guidance.
- Develop a course of action consistent with current written or oral policy.

☐ Review your course of action from the viewpoint of the official who will sign or approve the paper. Ask yourself these questions:
- Are all facts—pro and con—given? Are they accurately stated?
- Does the course of action represent a sound—the best—position?
- Can I justify my proposal if called upon to do so?
- Are all administrative procedures completed and accurate?
- Is the paper concise and clearly written?
- Would you sign the paper yourself if you were the supervisor?

☐ Realize that your paper may be modified by persons who will be asked to coordinate, approve, or sign the paper.

After taking the necessary actions above, you should:
- Determine who will coordinate and ensure that each has a continuing interest in the substance of the paper.
- Seek your supervisor's guidance, if necessary, to determine who should coordinate.
- Ensure that the coordinators' proper symbols are listed.
- Map out your coordination plan—"Whose signature do I get first?"
- Indicate your own coordination on the coordination copy of the paper before obtaining any other coordination.
- Coordinate the paper within your own department first.
- Face-to-face coordination is best whenever time permits or when the subject is complex.
- Coordinate by telephone when feasible.
- If a nonconcurrence cannot be resolved with the appropriate official, attach the nonconcurrence to the package, and submit a summary of the disputed issues to your chief. Show future coordinators the nonconcurrence.
- Provide copies of papers you originate to coordinators only when they request and require them. Save paper!
- Don't let coordinators write on your original.

"*Faster than a speeding bullet. . . . More pow-erful than a locomotive. . . . No shorthand?*"

THE SECRETARY

If you're looking for an excuse, *NATIONAL SECRETARIES WEEK* is the last full week in April.

Say it with flowers. . .or just *say* it.

JILL-OF-ALL-TRADES

Before we enter the exciting twilight zone of word processing, I thought you'd like to spend a few moments with that all-important person, the secretary.

Ever wonder what goes through her mind as she sits in that strategic location watching the high rollers scramble up and down the greased pole? I decided to find out. And before you label me a sexist, I know there are male secretaries out there; there just didn't happen to be any in my vicinity at the time of the survey. So, if your Jill-of-all-trades is really a "Jack," the shoe still fits. I surveyed experienced secretaries and asked them about those things executives do (or fail to do) that irritate them and that tend to reduce their effectiveness. The comments I received were revealing. Here is a composite of what the secretaries had to say:

On interpersonal relations:

- It would be nice if the people you work for could extend a little common courtesy to a secretary by not making critical comments about a mistake on correspondence in front of people from other offices. It really is embarrassing!

- Believe it or not, some individuals (other than your direct boss) not only expect but demand personal amenities, such as janitorial work, stewardess services, etc. This isn't so bad and is even nice for secretaries to do voluntarily, but these demands often come at a time when you are directly involved in typing projects or other priority work. It would seem just as easy, during those periods, for a person to get his or her own coffee or straighten the desk.

- How would you like to work for a boss who thinks you and anyone he (or she) supervises are beneath him in education and social status just because he is the boss?

- A plague on people who walk by the secretary directly into the boss' office after she tells them the boss has visitors.

- Make your secretary feel like one of the staff. Too often she is "used" for eight hours and then retreats to her private world. Communicate with her. Don't be afraid to set office policy with her. She can't read your mind, and she needs to know what changes are to be made before the little irritants become big ones.

- I am infuriated by people who can't say "May I" and who are obviously inconsiderate of other's property, including:

  - People in need of scratch paper who tear pages from my desk calendar. (I realize that these items are paid for by the organization, but *really!*)

  - People who use or take off with my last memo pad.

  - People who borrow my various schedules, phone books, dictionary, or other essential items and either get lost with them or leave them in another location when they are finished.

  - People who run off with my pens and pencils (when it's time to take a quick phone message, it's really hard writing with lipstick!).

  - People who write or doodle on my desk pad, my calendar, my books, other papers, me, etc.

  - People who drop cigarette ashes everywhere in my work area except in the ashtrays.

  - People who leave half-burning cigarettes or half-empty beverage cans or cups on my desk.

  - People who go in my desk drawers when I'm not around or even when I am around, even the lowest peon warrants some respect. (Unless it were an imperative situation, I would never go in your desk without permission.)

  - People who use my desk during my absence and leave it less tidy than I left it.

  - People who have sticky fingers that pick up and read paperwork on my desk that does not belong to or concern them.

On general administration. Here's another list of "neat tricks":

- People who bring in work and believe that their task is more important than anyone else's and insist that their work be completed immediately (and they stand by and watch while the work is being done).

- Holding a project until date due, then stopping the secretary/typist in the middle of another project to rush that project out.

- People who insist on arguing with you concerning procedures that everyone must follow (most people believe their case should be an exception to the rule).

- People who bring in routine work and insist on interrupting you to give it to you when placing it in the in-basket would be sufficient. (Such interruptions cause you to stop typing, place a caller on hold, or interrupt your conversation with another person in the office.)

- Often a secretary, while assigned on paper to one boss, finds she actually does work for many others as well. It seems there is always at least one individual who feels his work (all of it) is priority or rush; no matter what else she may be doing (even for your boss), she has to drop everything to do his rush job. If only those individuals could realize that when everything becomes priority, nothing can be priority or take precedence.

- People who make corrections, especially in *red,* on typewritten papers that could be salvaged with a neat, simple correction.

- People who disregard notices or other written instructions, especially those involving timeliness.

- A person who wants a project done "right now" and then doesn't look at it for days.

- People who give me special requests (not in normal line of duty, such as running errands and personal typing) that I gladly fill when I'm not busy and then insist that I do the same when I'm extremely busy.

- A boss who does not include the secretary in staff meetings and does not pass on info to her but holds her responsible for being aware of the discussions held in the meeting.

- A person who picks up distribution and removes action items but says nothing about it. Also those who take care of items on deadline but fail to let the secretary know (and are usually out of the office on due date). This sometimes causes another person to take quick action only to discover it was unnecessary.

- I think we all hate "crash projects" but realize they do occur. Rush jobs are always hectic for both the boss and the secretary, but there are times when a little more planning can prevent this. Bosses have a tendency to leave things until the last minute, and this causes short tempers and inaccuracies.

- A boss who couldn't care less about the condition of your office equipment. Nothing demoralizes a secretary more than having to face dilapidated equipment day after day.

Well, does any of that strike a sympathetic nerve? How about these: One secretary offered the following insight on editing:

Let the secretary type drafts until you are sure it is really ready "to go final." As a secretary, I take great pride in putting out a perfect product, but, after retyping it so many times because every coordinating office feels it must make a change, that perfect product becomes a chore.

Ever hear of job enrichment? It's a recurrent buzz word that simply means trying to recognize and take advantage of human potential. Although not many people outside of management academe know the buzz word, secretaries can certainly describe the need:

In connection with the boss who thinks typing is the limit of our ability—so many things are done the very same way, at the very same time every year, and, unless some new things of interest are thrown in, we can begin to feel stagnant. For example, one boss I had did every trivial thing for himself. I was not allowed to compose anything on my own. But his replacement was just the opposite (thank goodness). He would give me a letter and say, "Get this information and compile it for me." When he saw it the next time, it was ready for his signature. That helped to give me confidence in my abilities as a secretary and made me feel he had respect for my abilities.

Another comment with a slightly different twist.

Many secretarial job descriptions state that she will be expected to draft routine replies to correspondence. But, many bosses don't give a secretary a chance to fulfill this part of her job; instead, she will be called in to take dictation that consists of "A negative reply is submitted." This seems a little absurd when a verbal request to the secretary stating "Send back a negative reply" would have been sufficient and could have gotten the job done. Some secretaries are capable of doing a bit of staff work (others are not). The boss should get to know his secretary's ability. Most middle managers are afraid to give their secretaries any responsibility. In fact, though, almost all secretaries are capable of maintaining the continuity of an office during transitional periods.

And how about one last zinger from an individual who put her finger on a gross misuse of secretarial potential:

In 8½ years of civil service work, I've used my shorthand in only two jobs. If secretaries are hired as stenographers, then damn it, they should be used as such!

Do you suppose one of the reasons for this misuse of potential might be that we're not mentally organized to give effective dictation? According to the experts, giving dictation just requires a little practice, and it's a tremendous time saver. Well, I asked for irritants, and certainly got them; but there is a rose among all those thorns. The communicative theme running through almost all the secretarial comments was

Know our abilities, challenge our capabilities, and appreciate what we do, and we, like the other members of your team, will make an important contribution to the success of the organization.

A WORD ABOUT WORD PROCESSING

The last quarter of this century has seen the birth and phenomenal growth of a new technology centered in America's workplace. Desktop computers have sprouted like weeds in the corporate garden, and a new language was born—hard disk, floppies, spell-checker, grammar checker, OCR, CD-ROM, Bernoulli Drive, Hypertext, and so on. Executives at all levels, who never learned how to type, are now seen picking the keyboards of laptop or desktop key pads.

It's not clear whether cost effectiveness has actually been enhanced by all this high tech, but the research supports the assertion that microcomputers and word processing systems can save time and money *if properly managed*. Desktop publishing, for example, saves several steps in the writing, layout, and publishing process without a significant decrease in the quality of the final product. In many cases, in fact, the final product is an improvement over previous less flexible and more time-consuming methods of publishing books, manuals, newsletters, forms, etc. Regardless of the extent of word processing usage and the application of high tech to the office area, two vitally important realities remain.

First, no amount of technology can remove the human element at the creation or input end of the particular communication—be it a letter, message, memo, or report. If the creator of the communication doesn't know the ground rules for producing a clear, concise piece of work, then the machinery can do little to fix it. If you're the creator, you need to polish your act—which is why you've got the *T&Q*.

Second, no amount of technology can remove the human element at the quality control or output end of the particular communication. Someone must carefully proofread and edit that letter, message, memo, or report, which is a second reason the material in this book is vital to your success as a communicator.

Don't ever be fooled into believing that today's technology can convert a weak communicator into a competent one. And don't hold your breath—artificial intelligence is still a long way off, if it ever gets here!

• •

There is only one giant machine operated by pygmies, and that is bureaucracy.

—**Balzac**

• •

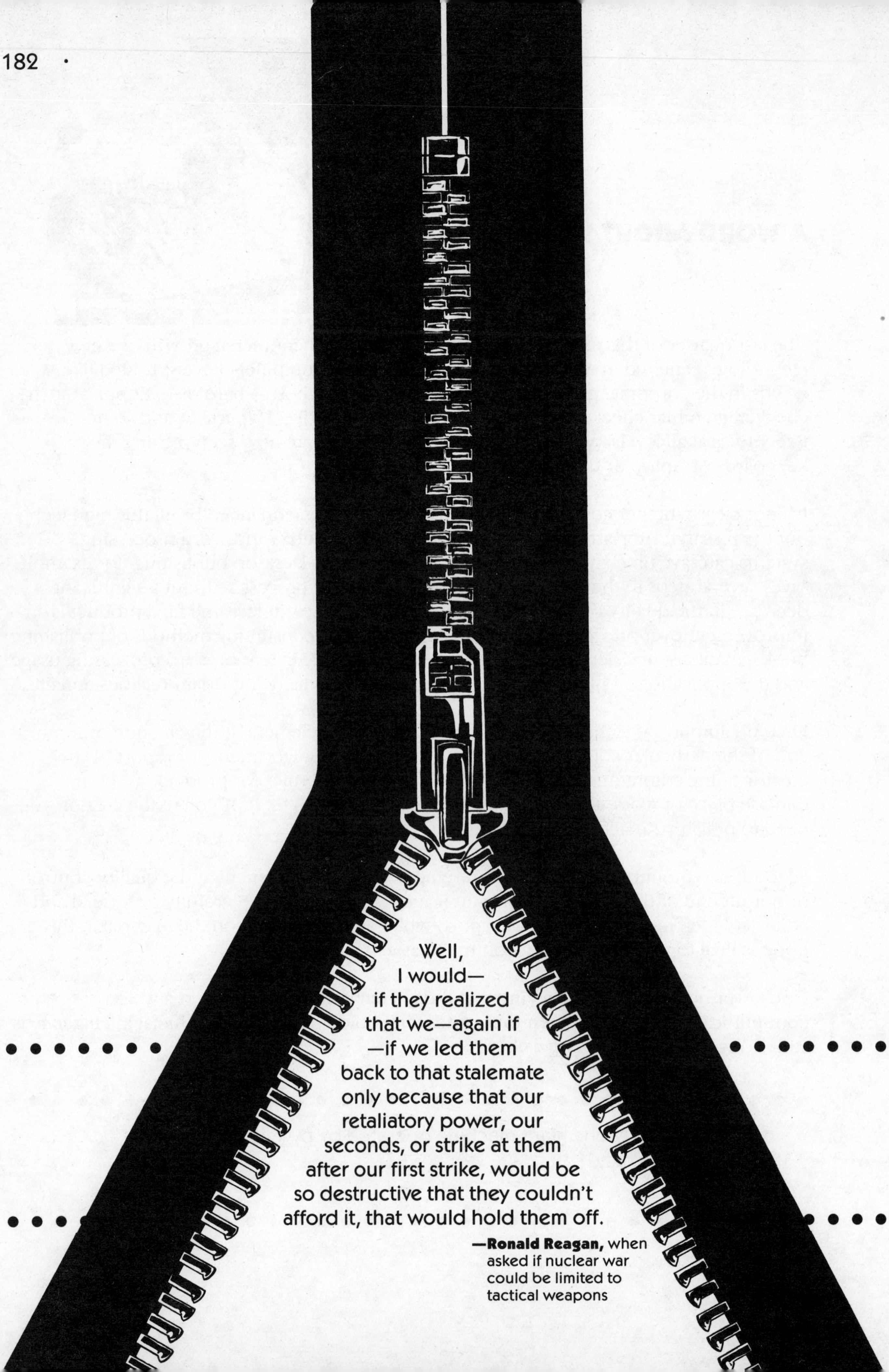

Well,
I would—
if they realized
that we—again if
—if we led them
back to that stalemate
only because that our
retaliatory power, our
seconds, or strike at them
after our first strike, would be
so destructive that they couldn't
afford it, that would hold them off.

—Ronald Reagan, when
asked if nuclear war
could be limited to
tactical weapons

CHAPTER 6

The Mechanics

or...How to
Avoid Ripping Your
Communicative Zipper!

HOW TO WRITE IT RIGHT

> **Punctuation marks is writer's rode signs they single stops starts pauses capitols also helps writers communicate his meaning to there readers**

Say what? The above is a mess, but with some effort, you could probably grasp the writer's meaning. But look how easy it is to understand that jumble when the proper mechanics are used.

> **Punctuation marks are writers' road signs. They signal stops, starts, and pauses. Capitalization also helps writers communicate their meaning to their readers.**

Proper mechanics (sentence structure, capitalization, punctuation, spelling, hyphenation, and abbreviations) enable you, the writer, to communicate more clearly to your reader. If you practice using the proper mechanics, you minimize the possibility of confusion.

This section is not a complete style manual. It's designed as a desktop, quick-reference guide to help you with some of the most common trouble spots and to encourage standardization and consistency. The rules provided are not all-inclusive, and they are not "the only way." There are many style manuals and writers' guides available today, and no two are exactly alike, nor is one more "right" than another. If your organization has a preferred style of using capitals, abbreviations, numerals, and compound words, use it. If not, this guide is designed to serve that purpose. For more detailed information, refer to a good dictionary and more complete style manuals on English, grammar, and writing.

• •

A foolish consistency is the hobgoblin of little minds.

—Emerson

. . .what better reason to occasionally split an infinitive.

—Schwartz

• •

PUNCTUATION

Punctuation marks are aids writers use to communicate a message clearly to readers. If used incorrectly they may alter an intended meaning, and if used excessively they can decrease reading speed and make your meaning difficult to determine. Although the trend in writing today is to use only the punctuation necessary to prevent misreading (*open* punctuation), there are still many writers who prefer the practice of using all the punctuation that the grammatical structure of the material calls for (*close* punctuation). I recommend open punctuation, but be aware that this style is not accepted by everyone and may cause you a redo here and there when you are writing for someone else's signature. Practicing good word and sentence structure will minimize the need for punctuation and may be the best method of alleviating a punctuation problem or question.

The following sentence is used to illustrate how different writers might punctuate a particular sentence.

If used incorrectly they may alter an intended meaning, and if used excessively they can decrease reading speed and make your meaning difficult to determine. *(Open punctuation—meaning is clear without using all the punctuation the grammatical structure of the sentence calls for.)*

If used incorrectly, they may alter an intended meaning, and, if used excessively, they can decrease reading speed and make your meaning difficult to determine. *(Close punctuation—using all the punctuation the grammatical structure of the sentence calls for—does not make meaning clearer and slows reading speed.)*

If used incorrectly, they may alter an intended meaning; if used excessively, they can decrease reading speed and cause confusion. *(A slight change in sentence structure—less words to read and the meaning is clear.)*

Punctuation should be governed by its function—to help communicate the writer's meaning. Therefore, use these writing aids in the manner that best allows you to communicate your message to your readers.

THE APOSTROPHE IS USED...

1. **To create possessive forms of certain nouns and abbreviations used as nouns.** Add an apostrophe and an "s" ('s) to nouns that do not end with an "s." Add only the apostrophe to nouns that end in s or with an "s" sound, and to the words "appearance," "righteousness," and "conscience."

the CEO's limo	Jones' family tree
OAS' president	our bosses' schedules
for appearance' sake	my boss' schedule

- To show possession of compound nouns, add "'s" to the final word.

    secretary-treasurer's report   mother-in-law's car

- To show joint possession for two or more nouns, add the apostrophe or "'s" to the last noun. Add only the apostrophe to plural nouns ending in "s" and "'s" to singular nouns.

    girls and boys' club   Janie and Jerry's son

- To show separate possession, place the possession indicators on each noun or pronoun identifying a possessor. Do not use an apostrophe when forming possessive pronouns; i.e., "ours," "theirs," "its," "hers," "yours."

    security guards' and janitors' uniforms

    king's and queen's jewels

    its paw was caught in the trap

NOTE: Don't confuse a possessive form with a descriptive form:

    your savings account (*savings* descriptive of account)

    your money's worth (*money* possessive of worth)

    the *Jones* survey (descriptive of survey)

    Jones' survey (shows ownership of the survey)

2. **To form contractions.**

   I've (I have)   it's (it is)   can't (can not)

3. **To form plurals of certain letters and abbreviations.** Make all individual lowercase letters plural by adding "'s," and make individual uppercase letters plural by adding "s" alone unless confusion would result. Make most abbreviations plural by adding a lowercase "s."

   dotting the i's, the three Rs   S's, A's, I's, and U's
   learn the ABCs   bldgs (buildings)

4. **As single quotation marks for a quote within a quote.**

   "Let's adopt this slogan: 'You can't take it with you.'"

5. **In technical writing to indicate the measurement of feet.**

   The room measures 16′ × 29′.

ASTERISKS ARE USED. . .

1. **To refer a reader to footnotes placed at the bottom of a page.***
   Two asterisks identify a second footnote,** and three asterisks*** identify a third footnote.

2. **To indicate the omission of one or more paragraphs.** Use seven asterisks and indent the beginning asterisk four spaces from the left margin; divide the remaining space as evenly as possible between the asterisks.

   *   *   *   *   *   *   *

---

*Asterisk: A mark of punctuation to indicate a footnote. As shown here, use no space before the asterisk and two spaces after the asterisk when used at the end of a sentence.

**Use asterisks with other punctuation as shown here. Asterisks follow the other punctuation mark, with no space before or between the asterisks and one space following.

***Number the footnotes if you have more than three.

BRACKETS ARE USED...

1. **To clarify or correct material written by others.**

   He arrived on the 1st [2d] of June.

   The statue [sic] was added to the book of statutes.

   NOTE: The word "sic" in brackets tells the reader something is wrong with the word immediately in front of the first bracket but the word is reproduced exactly as it appeared in the original.

2. **To insert explanatory words or phrases independent of the sentence or quoted material.**

   "Tell them [the students] to come to the auditorium now."

3. **To indicate you've added special emphasis (italics, underline, bold face type, all caps) to quoted material when the emphasis was not in the original work.** The bracketed material may be placed immediately following the emphasized word(s) or at the end of the quotation.

   "*She* [emphasis added] seemed willing to compromise, but his obstinate attitude prevailed."

   "Tell them to come to the gym *now*. [Emphasis added.]"

4. **To enclose a parenthetical phrase that falls within a parenthetical phrase.**

   (I believe everyone [including the men] will wear costumes.)

   . . .(including the men). . . [including the men]

   NOTE: If your typewriter is not equipped with a bracket key, use parentheses or draw them freehand (illustrated above).

THE COLON IS USED...

1. **To separate an introductory statement from explanatory or summarizing material that follows when there is no coordinating conjunction or transitional expression.**

   They ordered two books: *The Tongue and Quill* and the *Bible*.

   The board consists of three officials: a director, an executive director, and a recording secretary.

2. **When a sentence contains an expression such as "the following" or "as follows" and is followed by enumerated or illustrated items or when the introducing clause is incomplete without such items.**

   The new policy achieved the following results: better morale and improved relations.

   Results were as follows: better morale, less work, more pay.

   Consider these advantages when making your decision:

   1. You won't have to be somewhere at 8:00 A.M. every day.
   2. You can get more involved in community activities.
   3. You can pursue hobbies that you haven't had time for previously. (Note the capitalization and punctuation.)

3. **As a full stop with enumerations.**

   They selected two people: Mike Kozak and Tracey Gauch.

4. **With a quotation when the word "say" or a subtitute for "say" has been omitted, when the introductory expression is an independent clause, when the quotation contains more than one sentence, and when the quotation is typed in indented form on separate lines from the introductory clause.**

   The general turned: "Who gave that order?"

   The judge restated her ruling: "The defendant will remain in the custody of the sheriff until the trial begins."

   The speaker had this to say: "Please understand that what I say here today represents *my* opinion alone. I am not here as a representative of the company I work for."

The speaker said:

> The words you will hear from this stage today are the words and opinions of one man—me. I do not come as a representative of my company. I will not answer any question that is in any way related to the company I work for.

5. **To express periods of clock time in figures and to represent the word "to" in proportions.** *Exception:* Do not use a colon when expressing time on a 24-hour clock.

8:30 A.M.   0830 (24-hour-clock time)

1:15 P.M.   ratio of 2:1 or 3.5:1

6. **When expressing library references to separate title and subtitle, volume number and page number, and city of publication and name of publisher in footnotes and bibliographies.**

Mail Fraud: What You Can Do About It

10:31–32 (Volume 10/pages 31 and 32)

New York: Macmillan Publishing Co.

DO *NOT* USE A COLON . . .

1. **When the enumerated items complete the sentence that introduces them.** (Note punctuation.)

Liaison officers must

   a. become familiar with the situation,

   b. know the mission, and

   c. arrange for communications.

Not: Liaison officers must:

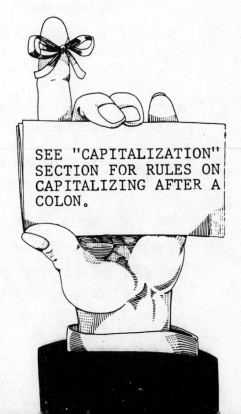

SEE "CAPITALIZATION" SECTION FOR RULES ON CAPITALIZING AFTER A COLON.

2. **When an explanatory series follows a preposition or a verb (except as shown in rule 4).**

> The committee members are Mary Clark, Linda Wilson, and Sandra Stephens.
>
> *Not:* The committee members are: . . . .

3. **To introduce an enumerated list that is a complement or the object of an element in the introductory statement.**

> Our goals are to (1) learn the basic dance steps, (2) exercise while having fun, and (3) meet new people.
>
> *Not:* Our goals are to: . . . .

THE COMMA IS USED...

1. **With the coordinating conjunctions "and," "but," "or," or "nor" when they join two or more independent clauses.**

> *Right:* The art of "creative accounting" is constantly developing, but twentieth-century technology has so speeded up the change that fiscal consultants now must run to keep pace.
>
> *Wrong:* The rapid expansion of the U.S. service industries ensures a continuing need for qualified college graduates to fill existing vacancies, and also ensures ample opportunities for advancement.

NOTE: The "wrong" example contains only one independent clause with a compound verb; therefore, no comma is necessary.

2. **To separate three or more words in a series, including the word before the final "and," "or," or "nor."**

> Will you go by car, train, or plane?
>
> You will not talk, do homework, nor chew gum in my class.
>
> We intended to travel to other countries (Germany, France, Italy, Spain, etc.), but we didn't have enough time.

NOTE: The use of "etc." is discouraged in running text, but when used, it must be set off with commas. Do not use "etc." when using "e.g.," "for example," or "such as." These terms indicate you are giving some examples; therefore, there is no need to imply there could be more examples listed.

3. **With parallel adjectives that modify the same noun.** If the adjectives are independent of each other, if the order can be reversed, or if "and" can stand between them, the adjectives are parallel and should be separated by a comma. However, if the first adjective modifies the idea expressed by the combination of the second adjective and the noun, do not use a comma.

> a long, hot summer (the summer was long and hot)

> a heavy winter overcoat (winter modifies overcoat; heavy modifies winter overcoat)

> a traditional political institution (political modifies institution; traditional modifies political institution)

4. **With parallel phrases or clauses.**

> Patients are classified as suitable for treatment at the crash site, as requiring medical evacuation, or as fit to continue on their journey.

5. **To indicate omission or words in repeating a construction.**

> We had a financial reserve; now, nothing. (The comma takes the place of "we have."

6. **To set off words, clauses or phrases that are not necessary for the meaning or the structural completeness of the sentence.** In many instances you can tell whether an expression is nonessential or essential by trying to omit it. If you can omit the expression without affecting the meaning or the structural completeness of the sentence, the expression is nonessential and should be set off by commas.

> They want to hire Fran Luckenbill, who has 2 years' experience, to run the new center. (The phrase "who has 2 years' experience" is nonessential information.)
>
> They want to hire someone who has at least 2 years' experience to run the center. (The phrase "who has at least 2 years' experience" is essential information.)
>
> There is, no doubt, a reasonable explanation. (This sentence would be complete without the words "no doubt.")
>
> There is no doubt about her integrity. (This sentence would be incomplete without the words "no doubt.")

In other instances, the only way you can tell whether an expression is nonessential or essential is by the way you say it aloud. If your voice drops as you say the word or expression, it is nonessential; if your voice rises, the expression is essential.

> We have decided, therefore, not to purchase the new computer at this time.
>
> We have therefore decided to go ahead with the project.

7. **With appositives (words, phrases, or clauses that explain, describe, or identify the noun).** If nonessential, they are set off by commas. If essential or restrictive in nature, they are not set off by commas.

> Our admin assistant, Miss Capouya, will handle the details.
> (Naming Miss Capouya is nonessential because she is our only admin assistant.)
>
> The battleship *Pennsylvania* was taken out of mothballs today.
> (*Pennsylvania* tells which battleship and is essential to the sentence.)
>
> Their daughter Rhonda won the contest. (In this construction, they have more than one daughter, and her name is essential to the sentence.)
>
> He lives with his wife Joanne in Atlanta, Georgia.
> (Strictly speaking, "Joanne" should be set off by commas because he can have only one wife and giving her name is nonessential information; however, because the words "wife" and "Joanne" are so closely related and usually spoken as a unit, commas may be omitted.)

8. **To set off interrupting words, phrases, or clauses when they break the flow of the sentence.**

    The faculty and staff, contract and in-house, are invited.

    The major, a recent promotee, is an experienced pilot.

    This, of course, was exactly what they wanted.

9. **After introductory subordinate clauses.**

    Since the school year had already begun, we delayed the curriculum change.

10. **To separate two or more complementary phrases that refer to a single word that follows.**

    The coldest, if not the most severe, winter we have had was in 1984.

11. **With transitional words and phrases, such as "however," "that is," "namely," "therefore," "for example," "moreover," "consequently," "on the other hand," "i.e.," and "e.g.," when they interrupt the flow of the sentence.** A comma is normally used after these expressions, but the punctuation preceding them is dictated by the magnitude of the break in continuity. However, when these words or phrases are used to emphasize meaning, do not set them off with punctuation.

    It is important, therefore, that we leave immediately.

    It is therefore vitally important we don't postpone the trip.

    She's highly qualified for the job; i.e., she has 35 years of experience!

    Debbie says she will attend—that is, if Art is invited too.

    Sailboats from a number of countries (e.g., France, England, America) will participate in the regatta.

● ●

Writing, when properly managed, is but a different name for conversation.

—**Sterne**

How forcible are right words!
—**Holy Bible: Job**

● ●

12. **To set off explanatory dates, addresses, place names, and words identifying a title or position following a person's name.**

> The date of the merger, July 21, 1986, was the turning point.
>
> We visited 10 Downing Street, London, England, in 1982.
>
> The address we shipped it to was 115 Birch Street, Middletown, Pennsylvania 17057, but it hasn't been received.
>
> Justin Robert Acreman, President of the United States, will speak to the council next month.

NOTE: Use two commas to set off the name of a state, county, or country when it directly follows the name of a city *except* when using a ZIP Code. When including the ZIP Code following the name of the state, drop the comma between the two, but use one after the ZIP Code number if there is additional text.

13. **To set off contrasting elements introduced by "not" or "but."**

> She is a trial lawyer, not a judge, and will be our new legal counsel.
>
> I am willing to go, but only if we stay at least a week.

14. **To set off statements such as "he said," "she replied," "they answered," and "she announced."**

> The pilot said, "Welcome to flight 409."
>
> She replied, "I have an appointment at 10 A.M."

If a quotation functions as an integral part of a sentence, commas are unnecessary.

> They even considered "No guts, no glory!" as their slogan.

15. **With the adverb "too" (meaning also).**

- When the adverb "too" occurs at the end of a sentence or clause, do not use a comma before "too."

  > You should try to improve your typing too.
  >
  > If you want to bring the children too, we'll have room.

- When "too" occurs elsewhere in the sentence, particularly between subject and verb, set it off.

  > You, too, can save money by shopping selectively.

16. **After introductory words such as "yes," "no," or "oh."**

    Yes, I'll do it.   Oh, I see your point.

    IN DESPERATION, THE CZECHOSLOVAKIAN MIDGET POUNDED ON HIS FRIEND'S DOOR. "THE RUSSIAN POLICE ARE AFTER ME" HE CRIED. "CAN YOU CACHE A SMALL CZECH?!"

17. **With afterthoughts (words, phrases, or clauses added to the end of a sentence).**

    It isn't too late to get tickets, is it? Send them as soon as possible, please.

18. **To set off long phrases denoting a residence or business connection immediately following a name.**

    Franco Franchini, of the Italian News Network in Milan, Italy, will be here tomorrow.

    Mr. Franchini of Milan, Italy, will be here tomorrow. (The comma is omitted before "of" to avoid too many breaks in a short phrase.)

19. **With introductory elements—items that begin a sentence and come before the subject and verb of the main clause.** The comma may be omitted if the introductory phrase is five words or less except when numbers occur together. If you choose to use a comma following a short introductory phrase, do so consistently throughout the document.

    In 1923, 834 cases of measles were reported in one city.

    In 1913 the concept of total war was unknown.

    In 1913, the. . . .

    Of all the desserts I love, my favorite is fried Camembert.

20. **To set off a phrase introduced by "as well as," "plus," "in addition to," "along with" when it falls between the subject and verb.**

    The faculty and staff, as well as the students, should be prepared to testify before the panel.

    The fifth and sixth graders, plus their parents, will be transported by bus.

21. **In the following miscellaneous constructions:**

- Before "for" used as a conjunction.

  She didn't go to the party, for she cannot stand smoke-filled rooms.

- To prevent confusion or misreading.

  To John, Smith was an honorable man.

  For each group of 20, 10 were rejected.

  Soon after, the meeting was interrupted abruptly.

- To separate repeated words.

  That was a long, long time ago.

  Well, well, look who's here.

- With titles following personal names. (Jr. and Sr. are set off by commas; 2d, 3d, or II, III are not.)

  Robert William Dunsmore, Jr.

  Henry Ford II

  Al Flateau 3d

  Donald Arthur Sitler, Esq.

  In text: Robert William Dunsmore, Jr., is. . . .

  But: Robert Dunsmore, Jr.'s car is. . . . (When you must show possession, drop the comma following Jr.)

- With academic degrees.

  James R. Macey, Ed.D.

  Dexter Harrison III, MBA

  In text: James R. Macey, Ed.D., will. . . .

- With names and titles used in direct address.

  No, sir, I didn't see her.

  Phyllis Kasover, you're not quitting the theater, are you?

  And that, dear friends, is why you're all here.

USE AN EM DASH (—) (-- ON A TYPEWRITER)...

1. **To indicate a sudden break or abrupt change in thought that causes an abrupt change in sentence structure.**

   He is going—no, he's turning back.

   Our new building should be—will be—completed by June 1988.

2. **To give special emphasis to the second independent clause in a compound sentence.**

   Our new pickup truck is great—it's economical too!

   You'll double your money with this plan—and I'll prove it!

3. **To emphasize single words.**

   Girls—that's all he ever thinks about!

   They're after one thing only—money—nothing else matters.

4. **To emphasize or restate a previous thought.**

   One day last week—Monday, I think—we had lunch together.

5. **Before summarizing words such as "these," "they," and "all" when they summarize a series of ideas or list of details.**

   A bat, ball, and tennis racket—these are what you need to bring for the weekend.

   Faculty, staff, and students—all are invited.

6. **In place of commas to set off a nonessential element that requires special emphasis.**

   There's an error in one paragraph—the second one.

   We will ensure all students—as well as faculty members—are informed of the President's visit.

7. **To set off a nonessential element when the nonessential element contains internal commas.**

   Certain subjects—accounting, calculus, and speech—are required courses.

8. **Instead of parentheses when a nonessential item requires strong emphasis (dashes emphasize; parentheses de-emphasize).**

   Call John Smith—the real expert—and get his opinion.

9. **In place of a colon for a strong but less formal break in introducing explanatory words, phrases, or clauses.**

   Our arrangement with the publisher is simple—we provide the camera-ready copy, and the company handles the printing and distribution.

WHEN USING THE DASH...

10. **With quotation marks:**
    ● Place the dash outside the closing quotation mark when the sentence breaks off after the quotation and inside the closing quotation mark to indicate that the speaker's words have broken off abruptly.

    If I hear one more person ask, "Where's the beef?"—

    Mary said, "When I get home, I'll— "

11. **With a question mark or an exclamation mark:**
    ● When a sentence contains a question or exclamation that is set off by dashes, put the appropriate punctuation mark before the closing dash.

    Please send the CEO's secretary—isn't her name Pat Stewart?—to the committee meeting.

    He's busy now, sir—wait, don't go in there!—I'll call you when he's free.

    ● When a sentence abruptly breaks off before the end of a question or exclamation, put the end punctuation mark immediately following the dash.

    Shall I do it or—?   Look out for the —!

THE EN DASH (–) IS USED...

1. **Before the source of a quotation or credit line.** Leave one typewriter space following the dash.

> We have nothing to fear but fallacy itself.
> – Herb Schwartz

2. **To indicate inclusive numbers (dates, page numbers, time).**

1987–90   pp. 25–31
800–0900   May 1987–June 1989

THE EXCLAMATION MARK IS USED...

1. **At the end of a sentence (or elliptical expression) to express strong emotion (surprise, disbelief, irony, dissent, urgency, amusement, enthusiasm).**

Congratulations on your new son!

I suppose you consider that another "first"!

Fantastic show!

2. **In parentheses within a sentence to emphasize a particular word.**

They call it a free (!) society.

You don't honestly believe (!) that, do you?

IN CONJUNCTION WITH OTHER PUNCTUATION...

3. **When an exclamation is set off by dashes within a sentence, use an exclamation mark before the closing dash.**

My new car—can't wait for you to see it!—arrives today.

4. **Use an exclamation mark inside a closing parenthesis of a parenthetical phrase when the parenthetical phrase requires an exclamation mark and the sentence does not end with an exclamation mark.**

> Our new car (a BMW 735i!) will be delivered tomorrow.
>
> The football game (Auburn versus Alabama) was a super game!

5. **An exclamation mark goes inside a closing quotation mark only when it applies to the quoted material.**

> Dot Powers said, "These rumors that I'm going to retire simply must stop!"
>
> You're quite mistaken—she clearly said, "Peachtree Café at 12:15"!
>
> Betty told her, "You had no right to say, 'Betty will be glad to help' without checking with me first!"

THE HYPHEN IS USED...

1. **To indicate the continuation of a word divided at the end of a line.** When in doubt about the proper place to divide a word, consult a dictionary and apply the guidelines on page 217-18.

> Use a hyphen to indicate the contin-
> uation of a word divided at the end of a line.

2. **When expressing the numbers 21 through 99 in words and in adjective compounds with a numerical first element.**

> Twenty-one people attended.
>
> Eighty-nine or ninety miles from here, there's an outlet mall.
>
> I kept a 3-year-old child while her parents were away.
>
> There will be a 10-minute delay.

3. **To link two numbers that represent a continuous sequence when they are *not* introduced by the word "from" or "between."**

> The instructions are on pages 15-30 of the enclosed brochure.
>
> She worked in the Pentagon from 1958 to 1985.
>
> The 1985-1988 period went by so quickly!

4. **To join single capital letters to nouns or participles.**

> T-square   U-boat   H-bomb   X-raying

5. **To indicate two or more related compound words having a common base (suspended hyphen).**

> It will be a 12- to 15-page document.
>
> She owns 2-, 10-, and 22-carat diamond rings.
>
> Long- and short-term money rates are available.

6. **To form compound words and phrases.** There's a growing trend to spell compound words as one word as soon as they are widely accepted and used. However, there are instances where the way you use a compound word or phrase will dictate how you write it—as one word, with a hyphen, or as two separate words. When in doubt, consult an up-to-date dictionary and apply these guidelines:

- Hyphenate words and phrases combined to form a unit modifier immediately preceding the word modified (except with an adverb ending in "ly"). Do not hyphenate these phrases when they follow the noun.

  > an up-to-date report; this report is up to date
  >
  > question-and-answer period; no time for questions and answers
  >
  > a $500-a-week salary; a salary of $500 a week
  >
  > a first-come, first-served basis; on the basis of first come, first served
  >
  > decision-making process; the process of decision making
  >
  > X-rated movies; movies that are X rated
  >
  > a well-known author; the author is well known
  >
  > a highly organized group; a completely balanced meal

- Hyphenate when two or more proper names are combined to form a one-thought modifier and when two adjectives are joined by the word "and" or "or."

  I took the Montgomery-Atlanta-Washington flight.

  He spelled it out in black-and-white terms.

  I want a simple yes-or-no answer.

- Use a hyphen to avoid doubling a vowel when the last letter of the prefix is the same as the first letter of the word (unless the dictionary shows otherwise) and when the second element is a capitalized word or a number.

anti-inflammatory	anti-fascist
semi-independent	semi-Americanized
micro-organism	ultra-atomic
pre-1914	post-World War II

- Use a hyphen in a compound word that sounds the same and is often spelled the same as another word but has a different meaning.

  recover (to regain); re-cover (cover again)

  recount (to relate in detail); re-count (count again)

  recreate (refresh); re-create (create again)

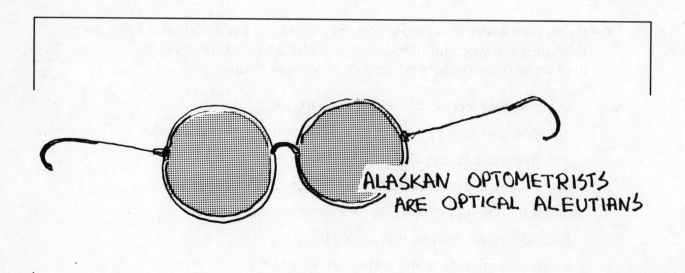

ALASKAN OPTOMETRISTS ARE OPTICAL ALEUTIANS

● To set off some prefixes and suffixes. Generally, a hyphen is not used to set off the prefix or suffix of a word, but there are some exceptions.

Non: Non words are usually spelled without a hyphen; however, use a hyphen when the second element begins with a capital letter or consists of more than one word.

non-Latin-speaking people	nonattribution
non-civil-service position	noncooperation

Like: Like words are usually written as one word, but use a hyphen when the first element is a proper name and to avoid tripling a consonant.

Grecian-like	gridlike
wall-like	lifelike

Elect: Elect words are hyphenated except when they consist of two or more words.

mayor-elect	president-elect	county assessor elect

Vice: Vice compounds are hyphenated except when used to denote a single office or title.

a vice president; vice-presidential candidate

the vice consul; vice-consulate's office

vice admiral; vice-admiralty

vice chancellor; vice-chancellorship

Well: Well compounds are hyphenated when they are used as an adjective before a noun; drop the hyphen when used following the noun. Well- used as a compound noun is always hyphenated.

well-made suit; suit was well made

well-known author; author is well known

the well-being of the family; consider her well-being

Ex (meaning former): Ex words are discouraged in formal writing; "former" is preferred. However, when you use "ex-" in this context, use a hyphen.

ex-governor	ex-AT&T executive	ex-convict

Self: Self as a prefix is joined to the root word by a hyphen. When "self" *is* the root word or is used as a suffix, do not use a hyphen.

self-made	self-respect	self-explanatory
selfish	selfless	selfsame
herself	itself	himself

Mid, Pre, and *Post:* Words with, mid-, pre-, and post- as prefixes (with a few exceptions) are written solid unless the second element begins with a capital letter or is a number.

midstream	mid-June	mid-1948
pre-Civil War	postgame	post-Gothic
preeminent	preexisting	preflight

Exceptions: pre-engineered; pre-owned

The ITALICS ARE USED...

1. **In place of the underscore to distinguish or give greater prominence to certain words, phrases, or sentences.** Both the underscore and italics are acceptable but not in the same document.

   U.S. monetary *policy* has been the subject of much debate.

   U.S. monetary policy has been . . . .

2. **To distinguish the names of ships, aircraft, and spacecraft.** Italicize the name only, not the initials or numbers preceding or following it.

   S.S. *America*   *Friendship* 7   C-47 *Gooney Bird*

3. **To indicate titles of whole published works in typeset material.**

   Writer's Guide and Index to English   *Phantom of the Opera*

( ) PARENTHESES ARE USED...

1. **To enclose explanatory material (single word, phrase, or an entire sentence) that is independent of the main thought of the sentence.**

    Our car (BMW) will arrive in the States today.

    The results (see Figure 3) were surprising.

2. **To set off nonessential elements when commas would be inappropriate or confusing and dashes would be too emphatic.**

    Wendy was named general manager of the Montgomery (Alabama) branch. (Parentheses are clearer than commas when a city-state expression is used as an adjective.)

    All the classes will meet three days a week (Mondays, Tuesdays, and Thursdays). (Parentheses are used in place of commas because the nonessential element contains commas.)

    I suggest you contact John Smith (if you want another opinion) and get his advice. (Parentheses used in place of dashes to de-emphasize the nonessential element.)

    Contact Rhonda Acreman—she's the YMCA's Head School Program Director—and ask her if their enrollment is closed. (Dashes are used in place of parentheses for emphasis.)

3. **To enclose enumerating letters or numerals within a sentence.**

    Our goals are to (1) reduce the number of curriculum hours, (2) eliminate the 90-minute lunch period, and (3) reduce the number of personnel needed to accomplish the mission.

    Please include the following when you file your travel voucher: (a) hotel charges, (b) meal costs (including gratuities), and (c) transportation costs.

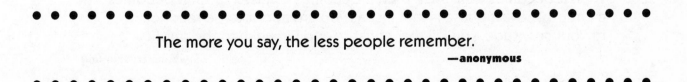

The more you say, the less people remember.
—anonymous

4. **To enclose numbers or letters identifying certain sections of an outline.**

1. xxxxx

   a. xxxxx

      (1) xxxxx

         (a) xxxxx

☞ ☞ ☞ Remember: In outlining, if you have a number 1, you must have a number 2; if you have a subparagraph a you must have a subparagraph b.

IN CONJUNCTION WITH OTHER PUNCTUATION

5. **If an item in parentheses falls within a sentence, place the punctuation marks comma, semicolon, colon, or dash outside the closing parenthesis.** Never put a comma, semicolon, colon, or dash before an opening parenthesis.

I'll see you later (probably Friday), give you the details, and collect your money.

I typed that paper (as I said I would); however, don't expect me to do another.

She says she cares about two things only (and I believe her): money and notoriety!

6. **Use a period before a closing parenthesis only when the parenthetical sentence stands on its own or when the closing parenthesis is preceded by an abbreviation containing punctuation.**

The results were surprising. (See the analysis at Enc. 2.)

Many kinds of flowers (roses, poppies, carnations, lilies, etc.) will be featured in the show.

● ●

Writing is an adventure. To begin with, it is a toy and an amusement. Then it becomes a mistress, then it becomes a master, then it becomes a tyrant. The last phase is that just as you are about to be reconciled to your servitude, you kill the monster, and fling him to the public.

—Winston Churchill

● ●

7. **Put a question mark or quotation mark before a closing parenthesis only when it applies to the parenthetical item and the sentence ends with a different punctuation mark.**

   The Pentagon (you've been there, haven't you?) is a fascinating office building.

   You've met Barry Goldwater (the senator from Arizona), haven't you?

   Morris said he would go. (In fact, his exact words were, "Going fishing? Of course, just as often as I can!")

8. **When using an exclamation mark or question mark to emphasize or draw attention to a particular word within a sentence, enclose the punctuation in parentheses immediately following the word.**

   You call this fresh(!) food.

   They said they will buy us four(?) machines.

THE PERIOD IS USED...

1. **To end declarative and imperative sentences.**

   His work is satisfactory.
   Don't be late.

2. **To end an indirect question or a question intended as a suggestion or otherwise not requiring an answer.**

   She wanted to know how to do it.
   He asked what the job would entail.
   Tell me how they did it.

3. **With initials and certain abbreviations.**

A.B. Henry	Mr.	pp.
John Q. Public	govt.	Enc.

4. **To form ellipses (three spaced periods that indicate an omission within a sentence, fragmented speech, or a pause).**

> The aim of assistance. . .human relief.
>
> "I. . .I don't know. . .I mean. . .can't go. . .I mean I don't know if I can go."

● Use four spaced periods (ellipses plus end period) to indicate an omission at the end of a sentence.

> Work measurement is the volume of work. . . .

● When a sentence ends with a question mark or exclamation point, use three spaced periods and the end punctuation mark.

> What work measurement tool was used to determine. . .?

● When a fragment of a sentence is quoted *within another sentence,* it isn't necessary to signify the omission of words before or after the fragment.

> Technicians tell us that it "requires a steady stream of accurate and reliable reports" to keep the system operating at peak performance.

5. **In vertical lists and outlines.**

● Use a period after each item in a vertical list when at least one of the items is a complete sentence. When the list completes a sentence begun in the introductory element, omit the final period unless the items are separated by other punctuation.

> After listening intently to the defense attorney's closing remarks, the jury was convinced of three things:
>
> 1. Several witnesses had perjured themselves.
> 2. False evidence had been presented.
> 3. The defendant deserved a new trial.
>
> After listening to the defense attorney's closing remarks, the jury was convinced that
>
> 1. several witnesses had repeatedly perjured themselves;
> 2. false evidence was presented by the prosecution; and
> 3. the defendant deserved a new trial as soon as possible.
>
> The following aircraft were lined up on the runway:
>
> B-52   F-15
>
> T-39   F-16

● Use periods after numbers and letters in an outline when the letters and figures are not enclosed in parentheses.

1.
2.
   a.
   b.
     (1)
     (2)

THE FELLOW WHO REMEMBERS WHAT HE WAS TAUGHT AT HIS MOTHER'S KNEE WAS PROBABLY BENT OVER IT.

IN CONJUNCTION WITH OTHER PUNCTUATION

6. **With parenthetical phrases.** Place a period inside the final parenthesis only when the item in the parentheses is a separate sentence or when the final word in the parenthetical phrase is an abbreviation that is followed by a period.

    I waited for 3 hours yesterday. (One day last week I waited 6 hours.)

    One other committee member (namely, John Henry, Sr.) plans to vote against the amendment.

7. **With quotation marks.** A period is always placed inside a closing quotation mark.

    She said, "I'll go with you."

8. **With a dash.** A period goes before a dash only when used with an abbreviation that contains periods.

    He was known as Anthony Jones, Esq.—and he was very well known.

● ●

A compilation of what outstanding people said or wrote at the age of 20 would make a collection of asinine pronouncements.

—**Eric Hoffer**

. . .he wrote that when he was 19.

—**Herb Schwartz**

● ●

? **THE QUESTION MARK IS USED. . .**

1. **To indicate the end of a direct question.**

   Did he go with you?   Will you be able to attend?

2. **With elliptical (shortened) questions and to express more than one question within a sentence.**

   You rang?

   For what purpose?

   Was the speaker interesting? Convincing? Well-versed?

   Who approved the sale? When? To whom? For what amount?

3. **After an independent question within a larger sentence.**

   The question How could that happen? went unanswered.

   How will we accomplish this task? is the next question.

4. **To express doubt.**

   They plan to buy us four(?) new typewriters.

   She's been associated with them since 1979(?).

IN CONJUNCTION WITH OTHER PUNCTUATION

5. **Use a question mark before a closing parenthesis only when it applies solely to the parenthetical item and the sentence ends in a different punctuation mark.**

   At our next meeting (it's on the 16th, isn't it?), we'll elect a new president. (Question mark used within parentheses because sentence requires a period at the end.)

   Are tickets still available (and can I get two), or is it too late? (Question mark omitted within parentheses because sentence ends with a question mark.)

6. **A question mark is placed inside the closing quotation mark only when it applies to the quoted material or when the same punctuation is required for both the quotation and the sentence as a whole.**

   She asked, "Did you enjoy the trip?" (Question mark belongs with quoted material.)

   Why did he ask, "What's that for?" (Question mark same as ending punctuation.)

   Did you say, "I'll help out"? (Question mark not part of quoted material but is the end of the sentence.)

7. **When a question within a sentence is set off by dashes, place the question mark before the closing dash.**

   The new course—isn't it called Creativity?
   —begins tomorrow.

"TAIL TO NAV, TAIL TO NAV... WHAT HAPPENED TO THE CENTERFOLD ?! "

• •

I am about to—or I am going to die: either expression is used.
—Last words of Dominque Bonhours, French Grammarian (1628–1702)

• •

QUOTATION MARKS ARE USED...

1. **To enclose the exact words of a speaker or writer.** A quotation must be copied exactly as it appears in the original, with every mark of punctuation, every capital letter, every peculiarity of spelling preserved. If the quotation is woven into the flow of the sentence, do not use punctuation preceding the opening quotation mark. When words interrupt a quotation, close and reopen the quotation.

    He said, "There will be a staff meeting in one hour."

    Why does she insist on saying "It just won't work"?

    "Since my car is in the shop," Bobby said, "I'll be needing a ride."

2. **To enclose slogans or mottoes.**

    He had a "do or die" attitude.

    "All's well that ends well" is a popular slogan.

    NOTE: To denote a quote within a quote, use the apostrophe as single quotation marks.

    Congressman Delaney said, "The interstate will contain a 10-mile section called 'The Robert Maxwell Memorial Highway.'"

    Sali said, "I really worked hard on that project and was delighted when the boss said, 'That's the best piece of research I've ever seen!'"

3. **To enclose words or phrases used to indicate humor, slang, irony, or poor grammar.**

    They serve "fresh" seafood all right—fresh from the freezer!

    For whatever reason, she just "ain't talkin'."

    NOTE: When using quotation marks with other punctuation, the comma and period are always placed inside the closing quotation marks; the semicolon is always placed outside the closing quotation marks; the dash, exclamation mark, and question mark are placed according to the structure of the sentence.

4. **With words and phrases that are introduced by such expressions as "the word," "marked," "signed," "entitled," "designated," and "classified" when the exact message is quoted.** Capitalize the first word when it begins a sentence, when it was capitalized in the original, and when it represents a complete sentence.

> The card was signed "Your friend."
>
> The article was entitled "Foundation Formed at IBM."
>
> The package was stamped "fragile."
>
> "Fragile" was stamped on the outside of the package.
>
> The report is classified "secret" and can't be distributed.
>
> Our organization received an "Outstanding" rating.

5. **To enclose the title of any part (chapter, lesson, topic, section, article, heading) of a published work (book, play, speech, symphony, etc.).** The title of the published work should be underlined (or italicized in typeset material).

> The final section of the quarterly report is called "Summary of Operations."
>
> When you read "The Quill" section of *The Tongue and Quill,* keep in mind. . . .

6. **To enclose titles of complete but unpublished works such as manuscripts, dissertations, and reports.**

> We need to get a copy of the "Congressional Report on Drug Abuse" as soon as possible.
>
> The title of his dissertation is "Smoking and Its Impact on Nonsmokers."

7. **To enclose the titles of songs and radio and television shows.**

> They sang "The Star Spangled Banner" before the game began.
>
> The "M.A.S.H." show is still being shown on TV.

8. **To denote inches.**

> 6 *"* x 15 *"*

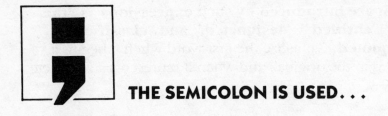

THE SEMICOLON IS USED...

1. **To separate independent clauses not connected by a coordinating conjunction ("and," "but," "for," "or," "nor," "so") and in statements that are too closely related in meaning to be written as separate sentences.**

   The students were ready and it was time to go.

   The students were ready; it was time to go.

   It's true in peace; it's true in war.

   War is destructive; peace, constructive.

2. **Before transitional words and phrases, such as "however," "therefore," "hence," "furthermore," "as a result," "consequently," "moreover," "nevertheless," and "for example," when they connect two complete but related thoughts and a coordinating conjunction is not used.** These words and phrases are followed by a comma.

   Our expenses have increased; however, we haven't raised our prices.

   The decision has been made; therefore, there's no point in discussing it further.

   The vice president had heard the briefing before; thus, he chose not to attend.

3. **To separate items in a series that contain commas (when confusion would otherwise result).**

   If you want your writing to be worthwhile, organize it; if you want it to be easy to read, use the informal style; and, if you want it to be interesting, vary your sentence and paragraph lengths.

   Those who attended the meeting were Dr. Cecil C. Robins, Dean of Curriculum; Dr. Albert L. Abernathy, Director of Student Affairs; and Dr. R.M. Doucet, Dean of Correspondence Courses.

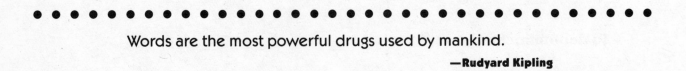

Words are the most powerful drugs used by mankind.

—Rudyard Kipling

4. **To precede words or abbreviations that introduce a summary or explanation of what has gone before in the sentence.**

> We visited several countries on that trip; i.e., England, Holland, France, Germany, and Denmark.

> There are many things you must arrange for before leaving on vacation; for example, mail pickup, pet care, yard care.

THE UNDERSCORE (OR ITALICS) IS USED...

1. **To underline titles of whole published works: books, pamphlets, bulletins, periodicals, newspapers, plays, movies, symphonies, operas, poems, essays, lectures, sermons, and reports.** Use quotation marks for titles of sections (chapters, units, parts, etc.) of published works and titles of unpublished works, such as manuscripts, dissertations, and theses. (In typeset material, italic type is used to indicate the titles of whole published works.)

> The <u>New York Times Magazine</u>

> <u>Time</u> magazine (word "magazine" not part of title)

> <u>Newsweek</u>

> I liked <u>Newsweek</u>'s article "Money, Credit, and Banking."

NOTE: Do not underscore a possessive or plural ending on an underscored word.

If Karl, instead of writing a lot about Capital, made a lot of Capital, it would have been much better.

Karl Marx's mother
Quoted in Alan Valentine's
<u>Fathers to Sons</u>, 1963

2. **To refer to a word as a word and not for its meaning.** You may also use quotation marks for the same purpose, but be consistent in whichever method you choose.

> The words <u>bored</u> and <u>board</u> are pronounced the same.
>
> The words "bored" and "board" are pronounced the same.

3. **To distinguish the names of ships, planes, and spacecraft.** Underscore the name only, not the initials or numbers preceding or following it. (In printed documents, italics are used for this purpose.)

> S.S. <u>America</u>   U.S.S. <u>Enterprise</u>
> F-15 <u>Eagle</u>   the <u>Columbia</u> shuttle

DIVISION OF WORDS AND PARAGRAPHS

WORDS

1. **Never divide one-syllable words.**
    friend

2. **Never divide words of five or fewer letters even when they are of more than one syllable.**
    ideal; *not* i-/deal   idea; *not* ide-/a

3. **Do not divide words by putting a single letter on another line.**
    around; *not* a-/round   military; *not* militar-/y

4. **Do not further divide words that contain a hyphen—break these words at the built-in hyphen.**
    self-/control; *not* self-con-/trol

5. **Divide words containing double consonants between the consonants only when they do not end root words.**
    permit-/ted, spell-/ing

6. **When possible, divide words after the prefix or before the suffix rather than within the root word or within the prefix or suffix.**
    applic-/able preferred over applica-/ble; valu-/able preferred over val-/uable;
    pre-/requisite preferred over prereq-/uisite

7. **Do not divide contractions.**

8. **When necessary to divide a name, carry over only the surname (never separate a first name from a middle initial, an initial from a middle name, or initials used in place of a first name).**
    Michael A./Brown; J. Robert/Grellman; R.A./Lee

9. **Don't divide surnames, abbreviations, and numbers unless they already contain a hyphen—then divide only at the hyphen.**
    Jackson-/Roberts, *not* Jack-/son-Roberts   AFL-/CIO   YMCA; *not* YM-/CA
    875-/2445, *not* 875-24-45 $55,000-/$65,000

10. **A person's rank or title should be on the same line with his or her first name or initials, when possible.**
    Mrs. J.H./Garman; Dr. James/Macey; Lt. Col. H.A./Schwartz

11. **When it's necessary to divide a date, separate the year from the day—do not split the day from the month.**
    March 16,/1988

12. **Do not divide the last word on the first or last line on a page; do not hyphenate the last word of three consecutive lines; avoid hyphenating more than five lines per page.**

PARAGRAPHS

1. **Never divide a paragraph of four or less lines.**

2. **When dividing a paragraph of five or more lines, never type less than two lines on either page.**

THE ABCs OF ABBREVIATING

ABBREVIATION: "A shortened form of a written word or
phrase used in place of the whole."

—Webster's Ninth New Collegiate Dictionary

What's the appropriate abbreviation? Can I abbreviate in this document? How do I write it—all capital letters, all lowercase letters, or upper- and lowercase letters? Can I use just the abbreviation, or must I spell it out? How do I make it plural—add an "s", or an "'s"? Where do I go for answers?

In the overall realm of writing and speaking, these questions are certainly insignificant, but to the millions of folks who prepare correspondence (especially those who write for someone else's signature), they represent minor problems encountered on a daily basis. To alleviate some of the fog surrounding the use of abbreviations, here is an explanation of the forms of abbreviating and some general guidelines regarding their proper use.

ACRONYMS

Words (usually pronounceable) formed by combining initial letter(s) of the words that make up the complete form. Most acronyms are written in all caps without punctuation, but some have become so commonly used that we don't even remember they are acronyms—we simply accept them as words in their own right.

SALT (Strategic Arms Limitation Talks)

AUTOVON (Automated Voice Switching Network)

scuba (self-contained underwater breathing apparatus)

laser (light amplification by simulated emission of radiation)

yuppie (young, upwardly mobile professional person)

BREVITY CODES

Combination of letters (pronounced letter by letter) designed to shorten a phrase, sentence, or group of sentences.

ASCU (Association of State Colleges and Universities)

DDALV (day's delay en route, authorized chargeable as leave)

POE (port of entry)

CONTRACTIONS

Contractions are shortened forms of words or phrases in which an *apostrophe* is added to indicate the deletion of letters or words.

don't (do not)   gov't (government)

wouldn't (would not)   cont'd (continued)

- Typically, abbreviations should be used in informal documents only, not in formal documents when style, elegance, and formality are important.
- Use abbreviations sparingly, correctly, and consistently.
- Spell out the word (or words) the first time used and enough times within the document to remind readers of its meaning.
- When there's a choice between using an abbreviation and contraction, use the abbreviation (govt. vs gov't). Omit the period with the contraction.

- When there's more than one way to abbreviate a word/phrase, use the shortest form that doesn't jeopardize clarity.

- Don't begin a sentence with an abbreviation (exceptions: Mr., Mrs., Ms., Dr.).

- If your organization has a preference on using abbreviations, find out what it is and *use* it. Otherwise, consult a dictionary or other up-to-date style manual for help.

- And if there's still doubt, LEAVE IT OUT!

CAPITALIZATION

CAPITAL FRUSTRATION

There is far too much time being spent by writers and typists trying to determine the appropriate use of capital letters (and abbreviations and numbers, as well). Everybody seems to want it a different way. Authoritative sources don't even agree! Put a half-dozen style manuals in front of you and compare the rules—two out of the six *might* agree in *some* cases. Why are there so many ways of using capital letters? Why do the rules change depending on where you work or who's signing the document? And why doesn't *somebody* establish a standard style of using capital letters?

The answers to more than one of those questions is simple: to allow writers a degree of individuality and freedom of style. Perhaps if we keep the *reason* for using capital letters uppermost in our minds when we write, we can alleviate some of this frustration.

The reason for using capital letters is to give distinction or add importance to certain words. "But," you might say, "I thought it was important and should be capitalized, but the boss kicked it back to be changed to lowercase letters." It's unfortunate, but if the document you prepare is being signed by someone other than yourself, that person has the last word. The best advice I can give you is find out what style your organization prefers and use it consistently. Even then, I predict there will be days when you "just can't seem to write anything right," and some of your paperwork will come bouncing back for redo. When this happens, don't fight it—change it; it's not worth an hour's debate or a ruined day.

Although the *T&Q* can't possibly cover every situation regarding capitalization, what follows is designed to provide some measure of help. You should also strive for consistency within everything you write or type. If you capitalize a word one place in a document, don't use the lowercase style elsewhere in the document. Many times either style would be acceptable—but not in the same document.

FIRST WORDS

1. Capitalize the first word

- of every sentence and sentence fragment treated as a complete sentence.

    Twenty-one people attended.
    More discussion. No agreement. Another hour wasted.

- of an expression used as a sentence.

    Really? No! So much for that.

- of direct questions and quotations placed within a sentence even if quotation marks are not used.

    The order read "F.O.B. Detroit."
    The insurance adjuster asked the question: How heavy will our loss be?

- of items shown in enumeration when a complete sentence introduces them.

    The White House advance team listed the following responsibilities of liaison officers:

    a. Become familiar with the situation.
    b. Know the President's route and schedule.
    c. Arrange for communications.

- in the salutation and complimentary closing of a letter.

    Dear Mr. Peepers   Sincerely   Respectfully yours

- after a colon when

    —the word is a proper noun or pronoun.

    —the word is the first word of a quoted sentence.

    —the expression after the colon is a complete sentence that is the dominant or more general element.

    —the material following the colon consists of two or more sentences.

    —the material following the colon starts on a new line.

    —the material preceding the colon is an introductory word, such as "Note," "Caution," or "Wanted."

    > Two courses are required: English and typing.
    >
    > When asked by his teacher to explain the difference between a sofa and a love seat, the nursery school boy had this to say: "Don't reckon I know, ma'am, but you don't put your feet on either one."
    >
    > Here is the key principle: Nonessential elements must be set off by commas; essential elements should not be set off.
    >
    > There are several drawbacks to this: First, it ties up our capital for 3 years. Second, the likelihood of a great return on our investment is questionable.
    >
    > They gave us three reasons:
    >   1. They received the order too late.
    >   2. The targeted bridge had already been closed.
    >   3. It was Friday, and nothing could be done until Monday.

- after a hyphen

    —when the hyphenated word is followed by a proper noun or adjective.

    —in a title or heading, capitalize all hyphenated words except articles and short prepositions/conjunctions.

2. Do not capitalize

- the first word of a sentence enclosed in parentheses within another sentence unless the first word is a proper noun, the pronoun I, the first word of a quoted sentence, or begins a complete parenthetical sentence standing alone.

    > The company finally moved (they were to have vacated 2 months ago) to another location.
    >
    > One of our secretaries (Mary) will record the minutes of today's meeting.
    >
    > The only tree in our yard survived the ice storm. (It's a pecan tree.)

- part of a quotation, slogan, or motto if it's not capitalized in the original quotation.

  General MacArthur said that old soldiers "just fade away."

- items shown in enumeration when they complete the sentence that introduces them.

  Liaison officers must
  a. become familiar with the situation,
  b. know the President's route and schedule, and
  c. arrange for communications.

- the first word of an independent clause after a colon if the clause explains, illustrates, or amplifies the thought expressed in the first part of the sentence.

  Essential and nonessential elements require altogether different punctuation: the latter should be set off by commas, whereas the former should not.

- after a colon if the material cannot stand alone as a sentence.

  All cash advances must be countersigned by me, with one exception: when the amount is less than $50.

  Three subjects were discussed: fund raising, membership, and bylaws.

THREE BLIND MICE
(translated for bureaucrats)

A TRIUMVERATE OF OPTICALLY DEFICIENT RODENTS
    OBSERVE HOW THEY PERAMBULATE
THEY ALL PERAMBULATED
    AFTER THE HORTICULTURIST'S SPOUSE
WHO REMOVED THEIR POSTERIOR APPENDAGES
    WITH A CULINARY INSTRUMENT
HAVE YOU EVER OBSERVED SUCH A VISUAL PHENOMENON
    IN YOUR CUMLULATIVE METABOLIC PROCESS
AS A TRIUMVERATE OF OPTICALLY DEFICIENT RODENTS

—from **Mother's Goosed Rhymes**
by **H. Alan Schwartz**

PROPER NOUNS/COMMON NOUNS

3. **Capitalize all proper names (the official name of a person, place, or thing).**

   Rome   Judy Kemp   Rio Grande River

   Earth   Joanne Horvath-Staley   Stratford-on-Avon

4. **Capitalize a common noun or adjective that forms an essential part of a proper name; the common noun used alone as a substitute for the name of a place or thing is not capitalized.**

   Statue of Liberty; the statue

   Panama Canal; the canal

   Washington Monument; the monument

   Potomac River; the river

   If a common noun or adjective forming an essential part of a name becomes removed from the rest of the name by an intervening common noun or adjective, the entire expression is no longer a proper noun and is not capitalized.

   Union Station; but union passenger station

   Eastern States; but eastern farming states

NAMES OF GOVERNMENT BODIES AND NATIONAL/INTERNATIONAL REGIONS AND DOCUMENTS

5. **Capitalize the full and shortened names of national/international governmental and military organizations, regions, and documents, except when used in a general sense.**

   U.S. Government; the Federal Government; government workers of the world (NOTE: Capitalize the word "federal" only when it is part of the official name of a federal agency or act, but not when used in a general sense.)

   U.S. Congress; Congress; Congressman Shelby, a congressman

   Department of the Air Force; the Air Force; Armed Forces; armed services

   Department of Defense (DOD); Defense Department

   U.S. Navy; Navy officer; naval officer

   U.S. Senate; the Senate; U.S. Senator; a senator; Senator James

   House of Representatives; the House

   U.S. Constitution; the Constitution

   the Capitol (in D.C.); the capital of Maine is. . . .

   The Reagan Administration; the Administration

NAMES OF STATE/LOCAL GOVERNMENT BODIES

6. **Capitalize the full names of state and local bodies/organizations but not the shortened names that refer to them unless mentioned with the name of the city, county, or state.**

   Virginia Assembly; the assembly

   Orange County Board of Health; the Board of Health of Orange County; the board of health will. . . .

7. **Capitalize the word "state" only when it follows the name of a state or is part of an imaginative name.**

   New York State is called the Empire State.

   The state of Alaska is the largest in the Union.

8. **Capitalize the word "city" only when it is part of the corporate name of the city or part of an imaginative name.**

Kansas City	the city of Cleveland, Ohio
Chicago is the Windy City.	Philadelphia, the City of Brotherly Love

TITLES

9. **Capitalize titles when they are used with a proper name or in place of a specific proper name; do not capitalize them when they are used in a general sense.**

   Cecil C. Robinsky, our Dean of Curriculum

   Have your director of research call me.

   Commander Wilkinson of the Royal Air Force

   John Kline, Director of Academic Affairs, Duke University

10. **Capitalize all references to a head of state or assistant head of state at all times.**

    President Herbert Hoover; the President's speech

    Our Vice President will. . . .

    the Queen (of England)

11. **Capitalize the names of departments within an organization, but do not capitalize the common nouns that refer to them.**

    Lynda Keene in Forms Management will design the form for you.

    I'm applying for a job in your Directorate of Curriculum.

    The vacancy in our directorate has been filled.

MILITARY RANKS

12. Military ranks are capitalized only when used with a proper name. Do not capitalize them when they stand alone.

Our speaker will be General Marshall; the general

We have 10 majors and 4 lieutenant commanders.

She's a staff sergeant in the Air Force.

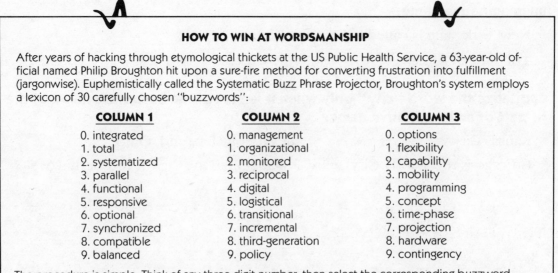

HOW TO WIN AT WORDSMANSHIP

After years of hacking through etymological thickets at the US Public Health Service, a 63-year-old official named Philip Broughton hit upon a sure-fire method for converting frustration into fulfillment (jargonwise). Euphemistically called the Systematic Buzz Phrase Projector, Broughton's system employs a lexicon of 30 carefully chosen "buzzwords":

COLUMN 1	COLUMN 2	COLUMN 3
0. integrated	0. management	0. options
1. total	1. organizational	1. flexibility
2. systematized	2. monitored	2. capability
3. parallel	3. reciprocal	3. mobility
4. functional	4. digital	4. programming
5. responsive	5. logistical	5. concept
6. optional	6. transitional	6. time-phase
7. synchronized	7. incremental	7. projection
8. compatible	8. third-generation	8. hardware
9. balanced	9. policy	9. contingency

The procedure is simple. Think of any three-digit number, then select the corresponding buzzword from each column. For instance, number 257 produces "systematized logistical projection," a phrase that can be dropped into virtually any report with that ring of decisive, knowledgeable authority. "No one will have the remotest idea of what you're talking about," says Broughton. "But the important thing is that they're not going to admit it."

THIS IS DEFINITELY A FOUR EIGHTY-FIVE!

COLLEGES, UNIVERSITIES, ORGANIZATIONS, COMMITTEES, AGENCIES

13. **Capitalize the proper names of colleges, universities, organizations, committees, agencies, etc., but do not capitalize common nouns that refer to them.**

> Loyola University; the university
>
> the National Security Council; the council
>
> Combined Federal Campaign; the campaign

ACTS, LAWS, BILLS, DOCUMENTS

14. **Capitalize the titles of official documents, regulations, directives, acts, laws, bills, and treaties but not the common noun that refers to them.**

> The Gramm-Rudman-Hollings Amendment; the amendment
>
> Social Security Act; the act
>
> Public Law 85-11; the law

NOUNS WITH NUMBERS AND LETTERS

15. **Capitalize nouns followed by numbers or letters with the exception of the nouns "line," "note," "page," "paragraph," "size," and "verse."**

Act 1	Appendix D	Part Two	line 4
Book 3	Attachment 2	Enclosure 1	Tab 2
Chapter 5	Table 10	Room 269	size 2
Figure 7	Rule 3	page 40	verse 3
Exhibit A	Building 888	paragraph 3	note 1
Task 3.1	Subtask 3.1.1	IRS Forms 1040	Book XI

PROGRAMS, MOVEMENTS, CONCEPTS

16. **Capitalize the names of programs, movements, or concepts when used as proper nouns but not when used in a general sense.**

> Social Security Administration; social security benefits
>
> Medicare Act; medicare payments
>
> Socialist Labor Party; socialism
>
> Civil Rights Act; a civil rights leader

COMPASS DIRECTIONS

17. **Compass directions are capitalized when they refer to specific regions, or when the direction is part of a specific name. Do not capitalize these words when they merely indicate a general direction or location.**

    - general direction/location: travel north on I-95
      the Eastern Seaboard
      the west side of town

    - specific regions: vacation in the Far East
      brought up in the Deep South
      visit Northern Ireland

    - part of a specific name: Southland Dairy Company
      Northeast Manufacturing Corp.

18. **Capitalize words such as ''northern,'' ''southern,'' ''eastern,'' and ''western'' when they refer to people in a region and to their political, social, or cultural activities; do not capitalize these words when they merely indicate a general location or region.**

Southern hospitality	Eastern bankers
southern nights	southern California
Midwesterner	Western Hemisphere
the Northern vote	northern Maine

Noah Webster's wife, returning home from a long trip, discovered the lexicographer ''in flagrante delicto'' with a pretty chambermaid. ''Mr. Webster!'' she gasped, ''I am surprised!''

''No, my dear,'' said Webster with a reproving smile. ''You are shocked; I am surprised.''

Henny Youngman

• •

Let a fool hold his tongue and he will pass for a sage.

—Publius Syrus

• •

DAYS OF WEEK, MONTHS, HOLIDAYS, RELIGION, RELIGIOUS HOLIDAYS, EVENTS, PERIODS, RACES, PEOPLES, LANGUAGES, SEASONS

19. **Capitalize the days of the week, month, holidays, religions, religious days, historic events, races, peoples, periods, and languages. Do not capitalize seasons.**

Sunday, Monday	the Great Depression
January; February	the Christian Era
Veterans Day; New Year's Day	Chinese
Passover; Christmas; Easter	Judaism; Christianity
Battle of the Bulge	African-American
World War II	Fourth of July; the Fourth
spring; summer; winter; fall	Negro; black; white

NOTE: A numerical designation of a period is lowercased if it's not part of a proper noun; i.e., twentieth century; the sixteen hundreds.

COMMERCIAL PRODUCTS

20. **Capitalize trade names, variety names, and names of market grades and brands, but don't capitalize the common nouns following such names.**

Snow Top orange juice (trade name)

Plexiglass (trade name)

Red Radiance rose (variety)

Choice lamb chops (market grade)

Ebony soap

Fizz-Cola; Fizz

Dictatalk Machine

Perfect Image copier

COURSE TITLES AND SUBJECTS

21. **Capitalize the names of specific course titles but not areas of study.**

American History 201 meets on Thursdays.

Rhonda is majoring in American history.

Psychology of Career Adjustment will be offered next quarter.

ACADEMIC DEGREES

22. **Capitalize academic degrees used following a person's name or when the complete title of the degree is given; do not capitalize degrees when used as general terms of classification.**

> a bachelor of arts degree (general)
>
> a Bachelor of Arts Degree in Computer and Information Sciences (specific title of degree)
>
> a master's degree
>
> H.A. Schwartz, Doctor of Philosophy

● ●

In composing, as a general rule, run your pen through every other word you have written; you have no idea what vigor it will give your style.

—Sydney Smith (1816)

● ●

NUMBERS

THE "WAFFLE RULE". . .

It is impossible to establish (or find in the literature) an entirely consistent set of rules governing the use of numbers—sorry! In general, numbers 10 and above should be expressed in figures, and numbers one through nine should be expressed in words. The exclusive use of words to express numbers is usually confined to ultraformal documents, and the exclusive use of numbers is considered appropriate in tables, charts, and statistical material. Since most writing is neither ultraformal nor ultratechnical, you'll probably use both figures and words in varying proportions. When expressing numbers, keep in mind the significant difference in the appearance of numbers. Figures stand out more clearly from the surrounding words, while numbers expressed in words are unemphatic, more formal, and they do not stand out in a sentence. Figures emphasize; words de-emphasize.

The following guidelines provide a recommended style of expressing numbers. Remember, however, that sometimes personal preference, organizational preference, and appearance may take precedence over these guidelines. If you (or your organization) have a preferred style, use it. If not, apply the following guidelines.

FIGURE STYLE

1. The following categories are almost always expressed in figures.

TIME:

payable in 30 days*   waiting 3 hours*

a note due in 6 months*   15 minutes later*

AGE:

a 3-year-old child*   a boy 6 years old

52 years 10 months 5 days old

CLOCK TIME:

at 9:30 A.M.   0800 (do not use
                             the word "hours"
6 o'clock (do not use A.M.   when expressing
or P.M. with "o'clock")   time on a 24-hour clock)

after 3:15 P.M.

MONEY:

a $20 bill $5,000 to $10,000 worth

$3 per pound   It cost 75 cents
                             (if sentence contains other
a check for $125   monetary amounts requiring the
                             dollar sign, use $.75).

MEASUREMENTS:

110 meters long   5,280 feet

about 10 yards wide   2 feet by 1 foot 8 inches

8- by 11-inch paper   200 horsepower

*Sometimes expressed in words in executive correspondence, especially when there are no other numbers used in the document.

DATES:

June 5, 1981	April 4 to June 20, 1988
May, June, and July 1980	21st of July
Fiscal Year 1984; FY84	Academic Year 1983; AY83
class of 1983 or class of '83	

DIMENSIONS, SIZES, TEMPERATURES:

a room 4 by 5 meters	a 15- by 30-foot room
size 6 tennis shoes	thermometer reads 16 degrees

PERCENTAGES, RATIOS, PROPORTIONS, SCORES, AND VOTING RESULTS:

a 15 percent discount	a 50-50 chance
(use % in technical writing, graphs, charts)	a score of 85
	Auburn 32, Alabama 24
a proportion of 5 to 1	a vote of 17 to 6
	a 5-to-1 ratio

NUMBERS REFERRED TO AS NUMBERS AND MATHEMATICAL EXPRESSIONS:

pick a number from 1 to 10	divide by 3
number 7 is considered lucky	multiply by ¼

ABBREVIATIONS, SYMBOLS, SERIAL NUMBERS, AND DOCUMENT IDENTIFIERS:

$25	paragraph 3, lines 5 and 13
No. 985	1 Enclosure
A.D. 46–48	Attachment 2
Genesis 39:10	pages 352–357

● ●

More than any other time in history, mankind faces a crossroads. One path leads to despair and utter hopelessness. The other to total extinction. Let us pray we have the wisdom to choose correctly.

—**Woody Allen**

If truth is beauty, how come no one has her hair done at the library?

—**Lily Tomlin**

● ●

UNIT MODIFIERS AND HYPHENATIONS:

5-day week	1½-inch pipe
10-foot pole	8-year-old car
110-metric-ton engine	

2. When a sentence contains numbers used in a related series and any number in the series is 10 or more, all numbers in the series should be expressed in figures (except the first word of the sentence if it is a number).

Six children ate 9 hamburgers, 14 hot dogs, and 6 Popsicles.

Our office has six writers, one secretary, and two editors.

NOTE: No number in the above sentence is 10 or larger; therefore, all are expressed in words.

3. Numerical designations of military units are written as follows:

Air Force units. Use figures to designate units up to and including air divisions. Use figures for numbered air forces only if using the abbreviation AF.

31st Combat Support Group; 31 CSG	Ninth Air Force; 9 AF
22d Tactical Fighter Wing; 22 TFW	Fifth Air Force; 5 AF
934th Air Division; 934 AD	

Army units. Use figures to designate all army units except corps and numbered armies. Use Roman numerals for corps and spell out numbered armies.

92d Infantry Regiment	III Corps
7th AAA Brigade	2d Army Group
2d Infantry Division	First Army

Navy units. Use figures to designate all navy units except fleet.

Task Force 58	Fifth Fleet

Marine Corps units. Apply same rules as army units.

4. Numbers expressed in figures are made plural by adding "s" alone.

in the 1980s	temperature in the 80s
four 10s in the deck	two L1011s at the airport

...AND 8 Champignons
(eight?)
(ATE?)

NOTE: To make plural a number that is used as part of a noun, place the "s" on the noun and not the number; i.e., IRS Forms 1040, but "file the 1040s.")

WORD STYLE

5. **Spell out numbers that introduce sentences. A spelled-out number should not be repeated in figures (except in legal documents).**

> Twelve people volunteered for the job.
>
> Eight children participated in the relay race.

6. **Related numbers appearing at the beginning of a sentence, separated by no more than three words, are treated alike.**

> Fifty or sixty miles away is the Alamo.
>
> Five to ten people will probably respond.

Related numbers in the same set are also treated alike.

> The $12,000,000 building had a $500,000 tower. (Not written as "$12 million" because of its relation to "$500,000.")
>
> We mailed 50 invitations and only received 5 RSVPs.

7. **Spell out numbers in formal writing and numbers used in proper names and titles in conjunction with serious and dignified subjects such as executive orders and legal proclamations.**

> The Thirteen Colonies
> the First Ten Amendments
>
> The Seventy-eighth Congress
> threescore years and ten

8. **Spell out fractions that stand alone.**

> one-half of the vote; but ½-inch pipe (unit modifier)
>
> two-thirds of the population

NOTE: A mixed number (a whole number plus a fraction) is written in figures except at the beginning of a sentence.

9. **Spell out compound modifiers and numbers of 100 or less that precede hyphenated numbers.**

> three 10-foot poles
> three 1½-inch pipes
> twenty 5-year-old children
>
> one hundred 1-gallon cans
> 120 1-gallon cans

10. **Spell out rounded and indefinite numbers.**

> the early seventies; but the early 1970s
>
> hundreds of customers
>
> a woman in her fifties
>
> the twentieth century
>
> nineteenth-century business customs

11. **For typographic appearance and easy grasp of large numbers beginning with million, use words to indicate the amount rather than 0s (unless used with a related number).**

$12 million

$2.7 trillion

2 ½ billion

$6,250 million

less than $1 million

$300,000 (not $300 thousand)

12. **Form the plurals of spelled-out numbers as you would the plurals of other nouns—by adding "s," "es," or changing the "y" to "i" and adding "es."**

ones

twos

sixes

twenties

fifties

The real purpose of books is to trap the mind into doing its own thinking.

—C. Morley

ROMAN NUMERALS

Roman numerals are used most frequently to identify the major sections of an outline. They are also used (in lowercase form—i, ii, iii) to number pages in the front sections of books. The following table shows Roman numerals for some Arabic figures.

I	1	XXIX	29	LXXV	75	DC	600
II	2	XXX	30	LXXIX	79	DCC	700
III	3	XXXV	35	LXXX	80	DCCC	800
IV	4	XXXIX	39	LXXXV	85	CM	900
V	5	XL	40	LXXXIX	89	M	1,000
VI	6	XLV	45	XC	90	MD	1,500
VII	7	XLIX	49	XCV	95	MM	2,000
VIII	8	L	50	XCIX	99	MMM	3,000
IX	9	LV	55	C	100	MMMM or M$\overline{V}$	4,000
X	10	LIX	59	CL	150		
XV	15	LX	60	CC	200	$\overline{V}$	5,000
XIX	19	LXV	65	CCC	300	$\overline{M}$	1,000,000
XX	20	LXIX	69	CD	400		
XXV	25	LXX	70	D	500		

DATES

1900–MCM or MDCCCC	1988–MCMLXXXVIII
1985–MCMLXXXV	1600–MDC

A dash above a letter tells you to multiply by 1,000. Other combinations of Roman numerals are derived by prefixing or annexing letters. Prefixing a letter is equivalent to subtracting the value of that letter, while annexing is equivalent to adding the value.

49 is L minus X plus IX: XLIX   64 is L plus X IV: LXIV

STRIKE A BLOW FOR FREEDOM!!

Are all these rules making you numb? Why don't we put some sense in this nonsense and take it upon ourselves as rational men and women to make our own rule that will let us win at this numbers game. How about . . .

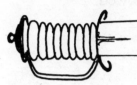

"Always express numbers as figures unless the number starts the sentence, or unless the use of figures would confuse the reader. . . or would look weird."

–Schwartz' Iron Law of Grammatical Bingo

The simplicity of it is downright ingenious. Think how many pages out of the inconsistent grammar books we could eliminate. Save a forest! Be a leader!

. . . a little review

Have you used *open* punctuation; i.e., punctuated *only when necessary* to prevent misreading?

Did you avoid the overuse of italics or the underscore for emphasizing words?

Have you avoided overcapitalization?

Have you written numbers in their proper form and been consistent throughout your document?

DOCUMENTING YOUR SOURCES

Documenting sources is an extremely important aspect of writing, but many writers are confused about what, when, and where they need to document. The rule is simple—if the ideas and information in what you've written are not common knowledge or do not represent your own work, you must document where and from whom the borrowed ideas and information came. ("Common knowledge" means facts of record that are widely known, easily obtained, and undisputable such as dates, locations, names, rules of punctuation.) As a writer, when you quote an authority word for word, paraphrase someone's thoughts, or use someone's ideas, model, diagram, research results, etc., you must show you have done so at the place where you do it. This is called citation. Citation, if done properly, fulfills a writer's responsibility for maintaining academic integrity. So, to keep yourself out of a literary (and perhaps legal) jam, give credit where credit is due, and cite those sources!

The following provides guidance on the use of footnotes, textnotes, and the double-number methods of citation. For more extensive coverage of these and other methods, consult more complete office style manuals. Remember, whatever style you choose for a particular document, use it consistently throughout that document.

FOOTNOTES

Footnoting is done by placing a number at the reference point in the text and typing the source information at the foot of the page. Type the number slightly higher than the line of text.[1] Then, at the foot of the page but no less than three line spaces following the last line of text, type all the footnote entries that are indicated on that page. (It gets tricky sometimes trying to estimate page length!) Begin the footnote entry by typing the footnote number on the fifth space from the left margin.[2] (This number can be typed on the regular line of text or placed slightly higher as done in the text material.) Single-space each footnote and double-space between footnotes. No bibliography is required for this method of citation, and the style for typing footnote entries is shown on the sample bibliography on page 244.

Examples

1. *A Guide to Graduate Study: Programs Leading to the Ph.D. Degree,* 3d ed. American Council on Education, Washington, D.C., 1976.

2. Galbraith, John Kenneth. *The Affluent Society.* Boston: Houghton Mifflin Company, 1961.

• •

The world is satisfied with words; few care to dive beneath the surface.

—**Blaise Pascal**

• •

TEXTNOTES

Textnoting is a means of identifying a source parenthetically at the appropriate point within the text. This method can be accomplished two ways: (1) by showing the source completely within the text (no bibliography required) or (2) by providing only the source's name and page number in the text and preparing a bibliography containing the complete source identification. When the bibliography contains more than one entry by the same author, include the date in your textnote to ensure the reader refers to the proper source.

The definition of analysis (William Marks, *Once Around,* Prince Books, New York, 1982) used is. . . .

The definition of analysis (Marks, pp. 23–31) used is. . . .

The definition of analysis (Marks, 1982, pp. 23–31). . . .

DOUBLE-NUMBER CITATION

This style of source citation is done by placing a double number at the point in the text where your source needs to be identified and preparing a bibliography. The first number refers to the same numbered entry in the bibliography, and the second number refers to the page number(s) within the referenced document.

With paraphrased material:
Enter (in parentheses) the number of the reference (as it will appear in the bibliography), a colon, and the page number from which it was taken.

> Providing no incentive (1:14) for the Soviet Union to strike the U.S. first in a crisis; i.e., Crisis Stability (1:7).
> *Or* . . . Stability. (1:7)

When the source is identified at the end of a sentence, the number can be placed just prior to or immediately following the final punctuation mark. Either way is acceptable, but be consistent—don't use both methods in the same document.

With direct quotations:

- When the quotation appears in the middle of a sentence, skip one space after the closing quotation mark and insert the source citation. The remainder of the text follows.

  > With his "Don't fire until you see the whites of their eyes" (3:36) statement, he turned and. . . .

- When the quoted passage falls at the end of the sentence and the passage itself is not a question or exclamation, the source can be cited just prior to the final punctuation mark *or* immediately following it. However, when the quotation falls at the end of a sentence and is itself a question or exclamation, the source citation must follow the final quotation mark.

  > Samuel Huntington, examining the conflict between military obedience and political wisdom, said, "Both the German officers who joined the resistance to Hitler and General MacArthur forgot that it is not the function of military officers to decide questions of war and peace." (3:77)
  >
  > *Or* ". . . to decide questions of war and peace" (3:77).
  >
  > He asked, "Why is it that careful analysis indicated that the military hero. . . makes a more successful political candidate than the man without military experience?" (3:157)

- Short quotations of five lines or less should be left in the text and enclosed in double quotation marks.

- Quotations of six lines or more should be placed two lines below the text. Begin typing on the fifth space from your left margin and end your lines five spaces from your right-hand margin. Block the indented material and do not use quotation marks (the indentation replaces the quotation marks).

- Direct quotations can also be handled by writing source identification directly into the text. For example:

  > Samuel Huntington, in his book *The Soldier and the State,* observed, "The outstanding aspect of civil-military relations in the decade after World War II was the heightened and persistent peacetime tension between military imperatives and American liberal society."

THE BIBLIOGRAPHY

A bibliography is an accurate list of all sources cited in the text from which you derived useful information, however slight, concerning the material you have written about.

According to Campbell's *Form and Style: Theses, Reports, Term Papers,* a bibliographic entry contains three parts—author, title, and facts of publication. The latter includes those items normally found on the title page—the edition number (if the narrative has been revised), place of publication, publisher, and date of publication. Armed with this information, a reader can find any of the sources you used in writing your material.

GUIDE TO TYPING A BIBLIOGRAPHY

- Use a blank sheet of paper and center the word "BIBLIOGRAPHY" one inch from the top of the page.

- Triple-space between the heading and the first entry. Number each entry. Single-space each entry. Double-space between entries.

- Begin each entry at the left margin. Subsequent lines are indented to begin beneath the fifth letter of the author's name (or title if there is no author named).

- Arrange the entries alphabetically by listing the name of the author in inverted order (last name, first name, middle initial). When no author is named and a title is used, initial articles—"a," "an," and "the"—are discounted, and the title is alphabetized by using the first major word of the title. (See items 10 and 17 on the sample bibliography.) If the title begins with a number, alphabetize as though the number is spelled out (i.e., 76 Trombones would be alphabetized by the letter "s").

- When two or more works by the same author are listed, do not repeat the author's name. Instead, a line five dashes long may be substituted for all entries after the first. List the works for the same author alphabetically by title. (See items 1 and 2 on the sample bibliography.)

- When there are more than three authors of a single work, the name of the first author is given, followed by the phrase "et al." (and others). (See item 4 on the sample bibliography.)

- Item 9 on the sample bibliography involves a coauthor and therefore follows the works written by the first author alone.

- For a book, separate each entry's three main parts (author's name, title of work, publication facts) with periods. The place of publication is followed by a colon, and the name of the publisher is set off from the date of publication with a comma. Underline the title of a book.

- Set off titles of magazine articles in quotes and underline or italicize the name of the periodical in which the article appeared. Follow this with the volume number, date of issue (enclosed in parentheses), and page number(s). (See items 2, 12, and 16.)

- Underline the title of a published report just as you would the title of a book. In addition, if there is no author, show the agency responsible for the report. The remainder of the entry is the same as for a book. (See item 10.) When an organization is listed as author, alphabetize by name of the organization. (See items 3 and 6.)

- When an interview is listed on a bibliography, include the names of both the person who was interviewed and the interviewer ("author" is used for the name of the author of the book or article in which the interview is listed), the place and date of the interview, and, if possible, where a transcript may be obtained. (See item 11 on sample bibliography.)

MECHANICS OF WRITING SOURCE CITATIONS

Enclose in parentheses the bibliographical number of the source, a colon, and the inclusive page numbers.

- Single source: (8:--) refers to the eighth entry in the bibliography and tells the reader you used the entire source.

- Single source; specific page:

    (8:45) refers to the eighth entry in the bibliography and tells the reader this idea is on page 45.

- Inclusive pages from the same source:

    (14:151–153) refers to pages 151 through 153 of the 14th entry on the bibliography.

    (14:1–2 – 6–8) refers to pages 1–2 through 6–8 of a document with double-numbered pages.

- Several pages (not consecutive) from the same source:

    (9:13,17,31,26) (Note there is no space between the comma and the next number.)

- Multiple sources cited at the same place in the text:

    (2:7–17; 14:2–4; 44:51) (Note there is one space following the semicolon.)

- Sources that are entire chapters, parts, volumes, figures, or tables:

    (35:Ch 5) (46:Vol 1) (15:Pt 3) (12:Fig 3) (Note spacing.)

BIBLIOGRAPHY

1. Anderson, Ruth I., "An Analysis and Classification of Research Results." Doctoral dissertation, Troy University, 1946.

2. -----. "Utilizing Shorthand Research in the Classroom." *National Business Education Quarterly* (March 1968).

3. Battelle Memorial Institute. *Strategic Sufficiency Force Planning Concepts and Relations, 1974–1984.* Columbus, Ohio: Battelle, 1972.

4. Brek, Horace R., et al. *Accounting: Principles of Application,* 3d ed. New York: McGraw-Hill Book Company, 1974.

5. Burchell, Robert W., and David Listokin (ed). *Future Land Use: Energy, Environmental, and Legal Constraints.* Center for Urban Policy, Rutgers University, 1975.

6. Committee for Economic Development. *The Schools and the Challenge of Innovation.* New York: McGraw-Hill Book Company, 1969.

7. Department of the Air Force. AFR 10-1, *Preparing Written Communications,* March 29, 1987.

8. Galbraith, John Kenneth. *The Affluent Society.* Boston: Houghton Mifflin Company, 1961.

9. ----- and Molinder S. Randhawa. *The New Industrial State.* Boston: Houghton Mifflin Company, 1968.

10. *A Guide to Graduate Study: Programs Leading to the Ph.D.,* 3d ed. American Council on Education, Washington, D.C., 1965.

11. Marks, Morton H. Interview with author. Montgomery, Alabama, May 2, 1987. Tape recording, Standard Systems Center, Gunter Air Force Station, Alabama.

12. Meyer, J. C. "The Synergy of the Triad." *Air University Review,* Vol. 2 (September–October 1971), pp. 17–37.

13. *New York Times.* January 2, 1984, p. 3C.

14. Quited, Charles E., Maj, USAF. "**Military Maneuvers.**" Unpublished master's thesis, School of Systems, Air Force Institute of Technology. Wright-Patterson AFB, Ohio, 1972.

15. U.S. Superintendent of Documents. *List of Public Documents, 1789–1989.* Vol. 1 of *List of Congressional Publications,* 3d ed. Washington, D.C.: Government Printing Office, 1911.

16. "White Water Fun." *Sportsworld* (February 1966), pp. 74–75.

17. "The Zebras of Africa." *Wildlife Journal* (June 1958), p. 3.

PROOFREADER'S SYMBOLS AND CORRECTION CODES

Where space permits, make editing symbols/codes within the text where possible to do so without jeopardizing clarity. Otherwise, circle the appropriate word(s)/phrase(s) within the text, and indicate the desired change in the margin.

MARK	MEANS	EXAMPLE
୨	Delete letter	spouses
⸺	Delete or delete/change word	any other day; any other day *time*
∅	Delete/close up	accommodate
⧻⧻⧻⧻	Delete underscore	we will all
¶	New paragraph	. . . today. Now
no ¶	No paragraph	
stet or	Retain deleted material	We must allow; we must
⌒	Bring together	yester day
＼	Join to word	the port
∫	Separate	box office
∼	Transpose	The word good receive
≡	Make capital letter(s)	United fund; Comtaff
∿ bf	Boldface	You can't go
✓ or lc	Make lowercase letter(s)	Basic RUles; BASIC RULE
⸺ ital	Make italic type	Time Magazine
rom	Make roman type	World War II
ds	Double-space	If you are willing, please share your views with us.
ss	Single-space	Everybody can improve their self-image. . . .

MARK	MEANS	EXAMPLE
⬭	Spell out; abbreviate; change word to a number; change number to a word	(AL) to Alabama; (Hawaii) to HI; (fifteen) or 20; one or ②
⟧⟦	Center horizontally	
	Center vertically	
⊏	Move to left	
⊐	Move to right	
⊔	Move up	
⊓	Move down	
↻	Move as indicated	
‖	Align vertically	
=	Align horizontally	
5⃞	Indent 5 spaces	
⊤	Right-hand justify	
✕	Delete entire paragraph	
—	Underscore	
∧ ∨	Insert	It is ∧ⁿᵒᵗ so
' or ∨	apostrophe	Bobby's truck
* or ⱽ	asterisk	The list is *
[ ]	brackets	the 1st [2d] of
⊙	colon	the following ⊙
, or ∧	comma	spring ∧ summer ∧ and fall
--	dash	It's great-fun too!
!	exclamation mark	You're kidding !
—	hyphen	self ∧ control

MARK	MEANS	EXAMPLE
( )	parentheses	The results(Table 3)
⊙	period	the report⊙Now we
" or ˅˅	quotation marks	She said, ˅˅why me?
; or ^;	semicolon	Move left;move right
#	space	She said,# "Why me?"
/	virgule or diagonal	data/datum

CORRECTION CODES

amb	ambiguous, make meaning more clear	
awk	awkward	
wo	change word order	
coh	improve coherence	
org	improve organization	
paral	make parallel	
frag	sentence fragment	
sst	sentence structure	
sp	spelling error	
sv	subject/verb disagreement	
trans	transition	
vt	verb tense	
wf	wrong font	
ww	wrong word	

IBID!!

LOC CIT!

ET AL!

SO'S YER OLD LADY!

SOURCES

Bartlett, John. *Bartlett's Familiar Quotations,* 14th Ed. Boston: Little, Brown and Company, 1968.

Blumenthal, Lassor A. *Successful Business Writing.* New York: Perigee Books, Putnam Publishing Group, 1976.

Bromage, Mary C. *Writing for Business.* The University of Michigan Press: Ann Arbor Paperbacks, 1971.

Ebbitt, Wilma R. and David R. *Writer's Guide and Index to English,* 6th Ed. Glenview, Ill.: Scott, Foresman and Company, 1978.

Felber, Stanley B. and Arthur Koch. *What Did You Say?* 2d Ed. Englewood Cliffs, N.J.: Prentice- Hall, Inc., 1978.

Fielden, John S. and Ronald E. Dulek. *Bottom-Line Business Writing.* Englewood Cliffs, N.J.: Prentice-Hall, Inc., 1984.

Fielden, John S. and Ronald E. Dulek. *What Do You Mean I Can't Write?* Englewood Cliffs, N.J.: Prentice-Hall, Inc., 1984.

Flesch, Rudolf. *On Business Communications: How to Say What You Mean in Plain English.* New York: Barnes & Noble Books, Harper & Row Publishers, 1972.

Geffner, Andrea B. *How to Write Better Business Letters.* New York: Barron's Educational Series, Inc., 1982.

Gibbs, Katharine. *Handbook of Business English.* New York: Collier Books, Macmillan Publishing Company, 1987.

Myers, Gail E. and Michele Tolela Myers. *Communicating When We Speak.* New York: McGraw-Hill Book Company, 1975.

Prather, Hugh. *Notes to Myself.* Moab, Utah: Real People Press, 1970.

Ranftl, Robert M. *R&D Productivity,* 2d Ed. Los Angeles: Hughes Aircraft Company, 1978.

Sabin, William A. *The Gregg Reference Manual,* 6th Ed. New York: McGraw-Hill Book Company, 1985.

Shertzer, Margaret. *The Elements of Grammar.* New York: Collier Books, Macmillan Publishing Company, 1986.

United States Government Printing Office Style Manual. Washington, D.C., 1984.

The University of Chicago Press. *The Chicago Manual of Style,* 13th Ed. Chicago and London, 1982.

Webster's Ninth New Collegiate Dictionary. Springfield, Mass.: Merriam-Webster, Inc., 1986.

THE INDEX

ABOUT THE AUTHOR

H.A. "Hank" Staley is a retired Air Force officer with a crazy-quilt history of experiences. The oldest of six childen, he performed in many community theatre productions throughout his teenage years, including commercial radio and television. After college and a successful foray in the field of marketing, he won a commission in the United States Air Force and liked it so well he stayed over twenty-seven years. He survived the Panamanian armed revolt of '63 (as a logistics officer), the campus antiwar riots of '70 at Southern Illinois University (as an AFROTC instructor), a tour in Southeast Asia (as a supply officer and squadron commander), and seventeen years as a tenured professor at the USAF's Air Command and Staff College (where he was director of research and chief of communicative skills). He holds a business degree from Miami University and a master of political science degree from Auburn University.

Depending on how the mood strikes him, Staley is or has been an actor, carpenter, businessman, corporate executive, retailer, landscape designer, briefing officer, speech writer, lecturer, teacher, curriculum designer, communications consultant, and award-winning author. His talent for helping people write and speak with greater impact has been tapped by organizations such as the City of Rochester, New York; the state of Alabama; School of Foreign Service, Georgetown University; Department of Health, Education and Welfare, Washington, D.C.; the Institute for Women Executives; and practically every military school and college in the Department of Defense.

Staley currently resides in Montgomery, Alabama with his wife and three sons who have no idea where his future interests might lead. He has threatened skydiving.

SCRIBBLE A NOTE TO HERB....

Jot down your ideas on how *Tongue & Quill* could be improved. All comments, large or small, complimentary or caustic, gratefully accepted. Send your comments to

"Dear Herb"
3322 Ridgefield Drive
Montgomery, Alabama 36106

To Order Additional Copies of

THE NEW TONGUE & QUILL:
Your Practical (and Humorous) Guide to Better Communication
by Hank Staley

ISBN: 0-08-035975-2   Price: $18.95

Credit Card Orders
(Specify Visa, Mastercard, or American Express)
Call Toll Free 800-257-5755

OR send Check or Money Order to

Order & Billing Department
Macmillan Publishing Company
Front & Brown Streets
Riverside, NJ 08075

Please add applicable state/local sales tax with all orders.
Shipping & handling charges applied to credit card orders only.
Allow 4 to 6 weeks for delivery.

Well, it's all communications, even the laughing. My last
bit of advice…probably the most important thing
you should remember…is to do a little bit of
laughing every day—at least when you talk to yourself.

—Otis C. Moore